PENGU
LEADERSHIP SHASTRA

Born in 1975, Pradeep Chakravarthy was educated in The School KFI, Madras Christian College, Jawaharlal Nehru University, where he studied international relations, and the London School of Economics, where he studied human resource development. He is currently pursuing a PhD on the administration of the Pandya kingdom. Pradeep began his career by working in the family business, the TVS Group. He later worked at Cognizant, Infosys and McKinsey. In all these organizations, he worked in HR and learning and development, with clients, to improve performance through behaviour change. For the past few years, he has specialized in conducting workshops, one-to-one coaching sessions and heritage tours that seek to impart leadership and life lessons from Indian history and philosophy. *Leadership Shastra* is his ninth book. His earlier books include ones on Thanjavur, Kodaikanal, the temples of Tamil Nadu and Ashok Leyland. His work on a children's history of south India and a translation work are currently in press. He lives in Madras with his twelve-year-old car and cricket-crazy son, Raghavan, and his father.

PRAISE FOR THE BOOK

'Heroes or villains, historical characters provide deep insights into how leaders take crucial decisions that impact the course of history—albeit not always in ways that they had imagined. Pradeep's book, written in an easy, approachable style, looks at how different leaders through Indian history dealt with difficult trade-offs, motivated subordinates and attempted to achieve their aims. Importantly, he includes the failures, such as the later Mughals, which as an understanding of leadership failure are just as important'—Sanjeev Sanyal, economist and writer

'History seldom reveals itself when it is happening. A clearer view emerges only in retrospect. Pradeep Chakravarthy has carefully chosen a few historical figures to show how individuals make history, and what we can learn from them. The lessons have a meaningful impact on the conduct of our actions and businesses. His erudition, his unbiased approach to history, his choice of the historical characters and their possible impact on our day-to-day actions make for very meaningful reading'—Suresh Krishna, chairman, TVS & Sons Limited

'*Leadership Shastra* should be required reading for everyone aspiring to be a better leader. Research-based accounts of leadership role models from Indian history are rare. Pradeep draws on his scholarship and passion to fill this critical gap and provides valuable and timely learnings for all students of leadership'—Dr Pramath Raj Sinha, founding dean, ISB, and founder and trustee, Ashoka University

LEADERSHIP SHASTRA

Lessons from Indian History

PRADEEP CHAKRAVARTHY

BUSINESS

An imprint of Penguin Random House

PENGUIN BUSINESS

USA | Canada | UK | Ireland | Australia
New Zealand | India | South Africa | China

Penguin Business is part of the Penguin Random House group of companies whose addresses can be found at global.penguinrandomhouse.com

Published by Penguin Random House India Pvt. Ltd
4th Floor, Capital Tower 1, MG Road,
Gurugram 122 002, Haryana, India

First published in Westland Business, an imprint of Westland Publications Private Limited, 2021
Published in Penguin Business by Penguin Random House India 2022

Copyright © Pradeep Chakravarthy 2021

All rights reserved

10 9 8 7 6 5 4 3 2 1

The views and opinions expressed in this book are the author's own and the facts are as reported by him which have been verified to the extent possible, and the publishers are not in any way liable for the same.

ISBN 9780143459071

Typeset by SÜRYA, New Delhi
Printed at Thomson Press India Ltd, New Delhi

This book is sold subject to the condition that it shall not, by way of trade or otherwise, be lent, resold, hired out, or otherwise circulated without the publisher's prior consent in any form of binding or cover other than that in which it is published and without a similar condition including this condition being imposed on the subsequent purchaser.

www.penguin.co.in

The Yaksha asked, 'Tell me, what it the greatest wonder in this world?'
Yudhishtra replied,
'Day after day, countless beings are going to Yama Loka.
Yet, those who remain, are convinced they are immortal.
What can be a greater wonder than that?'

CONTENTS

Setting the Context ix

ACCOUNTS OF THE WEST

Malik Ambar 3
The Deccan Sultanates 12
Chhatrapati Shivaji 17
Ahilyabai Holkar 32

NARRATIVES FROM THE NORTH

Babur 41
Jahanara 51
Aurangzeb 59
The First Five Sikh Gurus 72

STORIES FROM THE SOUTH

Marthanda Varma 85
Tipu Sultan 95
Serfoji II of Thanjavur 106

CHRONICLES OF THE EAST

Sankaradeva 117
The Ahoms of Assam 126

LEADERS WHO DID NOT ENLARGE THEIR LEGACY

    Osman Ali Khan of Hyderabad   135
    The Mughals after Aurangzeb   140

Broad Conclusions   148

A Word of Thanks   152

SETTING THE CONTEXT

History is a compulsory subject in school and given my own interest in the subject, I have often asked many people what they felt about learning history.

The replies have been of two kinds.

A few liked it, because they had a teacher who made it dramatic and real for them in class. 'The teacher brought the whole battle alive in front of us. I don't remember much of it, but I remember being very spellbound' was one response. In this instance, the storytelling of the person seemed to have injected a sense of drama into the subject and that is a fond memory. So, what did you learn from it, was my usual follow-up question. 'Oh, that I can't remember but it was interesting' is often the reply. Here, the teacher did make the subject interesting but it appears that there was no connection made to history as far as the person's life was concerned. Little was perhaps done to make it relevant to the present day.

Many people's response was that they found the subject boring. The dates, the battles, the many details all seemed meaningless. They studied it because they had to but always asked themselves, 'What is the point of reading all this? I am never going to use this.' Here, devoid of the storytelling, not only did the subject lose its entertainment value but it also lost its relevance itself. This sort of reply was usual.

For me, though, history was different.

Growing up in the 1980s, I spent every summer with my maternal grandparents in a home spread over 10,000 sq. ft. in a small town called Palayamkottai in Tamil Nadu. The home had been in our family for five generations. It was spread across two adjacent streets. In addition to the 10,000 sq. ft. of built-up area was a wild garden with many trees and many more snakes.

The family practice was that whenever something became unfit for use, it was thrown upstairs into four large rooms (about 5,000 sq. ft. with 25-foot-high ceilings). Old clothes, textbooks, notebooks, furniture, vessels and household articles, even newspapers and magazines, all found their way up rather than out through the dustbin. In the afternoons when the elders slept, I was banished to this magical land of the past and could do whatever I wanted so long as I did not wake up the sleeping adults downstairs. Poring through the remnants of the past of my uncles and aunts and ancestors (every couple seemed to have a minimum of five children who had many more offspring) and all their things, I was struck by the similarities. Their doodles on the textbooks were similar to mine and their subjects similar even if the textbooks were different. I loved listening to my grandfather's stories in the night and my grandfather remembered listening to his great-grandfather telling him stories when he was young!

I realised that in history, at least some of it repeats itself often. For example, many of my ancestors did not particularly care for maths like me. I could relate to that. But the language of their textbooks and their clothes were things I could not connect to.

Two decades later, after a visit to the Tirumeyyam cave temples, I wanted to find books on the temples. A friend directed me to the library of the State Archaeological Survey of India. A librarian there gave me a book on the English translations of the inscriptions. Those inscriptions were, incidentally, a thousand years old—a fact that I had not observed. One of them spoke about a bitter caste dispute that was settled on 7 May 1245 CE by partitioning the village with a dividing wall. Today, the village has no wall, very few pilgrims and hardly anyone from the castes that fought so bitterly and bloodily. I wrote an article about this and it was published in *The Hindu*, which for any long-term Madrasi / Chennaiite is as good if not better than the Nobel Prize!

They told me they loved the social rather than religious flavour I had given to the article. Writing more such articles, embarking on a PhD and a chance conversation with Devdutt Pattanaik made me see a pattern in every one of the 30,000+ lines of inscriptions I had read by then. All of them were either about a conflict being resolved or a person leaving (through a gift) a legacy for posterity. Years of work with organisations in human resources (HR), learning and development (L & D) and consulting had the same flavour—conflicts and interpersonal issues that needed sorting and supporting others to leave behind a legacy for the future.

The idea for this book was born as a result of these experiences. The underlying thought was what is that we could learn from history.

My childhood, my lifelong interest in history and a desire to bring personal passion and professional work together has breathed life into this book.

How history can be useful to you

Today, you don't need to go in search of history—it finds you through social media and WhatsApp! How much of it is genuine is another discussion but, unlike in the past when you had to pick up a book to read about history, history-writing in the present day has many formats that appeal to different people. However much we liked or disliked history, having learnt it in school, there is something we remember from it.

In addition to the history of a region, we have full and ready access to our own history and that of those around us—friends, family, the institutions we are connected to and the area we live in. In a manner of speaking, history is all around us in multiple layers and depths. With ready (and free!) access, is it not a smart thing to use history to improve the one thing we are all doing from the moment we are conceived till the moment we die—performance?!

At home or at work we are constantly performing—to meet targets, to live up to expectation set by others or us and so on. How can we use this readily and freely available knowledge of history to help us perform better? If we can use this free resource to help us, that could mean an increase in income, time-saving or just happiness from deeper relationships. Surely the reward is worth the effort and the cost.

However, to smartly use this history of our lives or those of others, we need to have a special lens. This is free too—you don't need to buy it online. It is just a magical question that you need to ask. When you ask the question, it opens up all the different stories in history and channels it into information that you can use. You can benefit from it just the way I have been able to and use it to achieve any of your goals and enjoy the monetary or non-monetary rewards that come with it. The effort is tiny compared to the benefits.

How can you make history work for you?

As technology converts our world into webs of interconnected systems that are more and more complex, as individuals we can only see smaller and smaller parts of the whole. How we learn becomes a strong indicator of how we can perform. Because of the interconnectedness, the more we learn from domains not our own, the more likely it is we will be able to innovate and think out of the box. Today's world has rapidly changing rules, and learning from history can provide a powerful tool for complementing machines that can now do all the simple repetitive tasks.

Thinking like this and using history to improve your performance will not be easy. In the short term, you will find this hard, even taxing or boring. However, this way of learning about yourself from the past, and from other leaders and your own past, is a desirable difficulty—obstacles that make learning more challenging, slower and frustrating in the short term but better in the long term.

The key lens to have is to temporarily strip history of the dates and chronology. This may sound like sacrilege. Before you judge me, remember that our limited purpose now is to make history help us improve our performance. You can bring back the dates later, but when you strip the dates away, you are left with the actions of people.

Let us now work with a set of actions. For example, draw up a list of actions a king performed. This may be easy to list. But be aware, as you are listing, of resisting your temptation into classifying them into 'good' and 'bad'. We are not here to judge and pronounce a judgement on the king. The poor chap has been dead and gone for centuries! Let us not waste our time judging and focus on how to use his actions to benefit our performance. So be a little selfish here. To reiterate, the focus is on using history to improve your own performance.

Now that we have a list of actions, we have to ask the tough question, the 'key' as it were to open history to make it useful to us. That question is simply: 'What may have been his/her needs in doing what he did?' Needs here can be physical (air, food, water, a house), emotional (affection, collaboration) or intellectual (respect, independence, adventure).

When you read through the life of actions of the king, we can speculate what needs the person would have had. Based on this analysis, we can ask ourselves how much of that need was met—in the short term when the king lived and in the long term which could be his last years or after him.

Yes, contexts always change. The kings of the past did not have technology or information overload to deal with it, but the premise here is that fundamental human nature—of our deepest needs and our fears (what we feel when a need is not met)—has not only been the same in the past or present but will be so in the future as well.

The more you read and understand history, the more you realise that human nature in terms of needs and fears are eternal and universal. Context matters but strip away the judgements, the biases and the noise (dates and chronology) and read the story of your past or the past of others from the lens of human nature. Ask the following questions:

- What were the needs and fears that motivated them to do what they did?
- What was the short-term and long-term effect of their actions?
- Did they get what they want?

Then we can ask the question that is much easier for us today—what's in it for me? From their needs and the way they achieved them, in my limited circle of what can I influence, what can I start, stop or continue so that I can achieve my needs in the short term and the long term.

Some pitfalls to guard against:

- Focus on the possible needs and fears. There are lists available online if you want. Keep one handy. Remember that one action can be because of multiple needs.
- Constantly be aware and resist the temptation to judge

'good' and 'bad'. That will take you away from your goal of using history to improve your own performance. The historical information we have may also have biases. Collect as much as you can from varied sources to minimise it. Bias can never be eliminated but we can be watchful to not let it affect us.

- Related to the above, be mindful of not branding any historical personalities as 'good' or 'bad'. As our epics teach us, humans are a complex mix of qualities, and good and bad are very relative to time, space and person.

There is always a lesson from a historical anecdote on what you can start or stop or continue to do. If you can't find one, you aren't looking hard enough!

Finally, it is all about action. Once you have made the connection, look for short, simple actions that you can take and that can tell other people that you have indeed learnt something. Here too, the start-stop-continue format can help you sharpen your action into something that is measurable, observable and time-bound.

How this book is structured

Each chapter is structured around a historical personality (sometimes more than one personality) and what we can learn from him/her/them. I have tried to draw business and personal lessons from accounts of their lives and how their lives can serve as prompts to get us to reflect on our own lives, careers and organisations. In addition, I have attempted to pose questions at the end of each chapter in order to enable the reader to carry out this exercise beyond the confines of this book.

If you want a more structured way of using the book, read the concluding chapter section entitled 'Sadhana' first and then navigate through the main chapters. It is perfectly all right, though, to read each chapter and find your own way to apply insights from history to improve your performance.

My purpose in writing this book is to help you recognise that history need not be a boring or irrelevant subject. It can instead be a cost-effective and energy-efficient way to improve your performance.

It can be very relevant for you to understand yourself and change the way you react to the world around you. For that you need to:

a. Start seeing historical personalities as having needs and fears that are very similar to yours.
b. Recognise how they achieved their goals and learn what worked/did not work in their lifetime and beyond.
c. Recognise from your own life history where you have also displayed such needs/fears/actions.
d. Work to link Indian history and your personal history insights to create small behaviours that can change your performance.

Of course, your need might be completely different from all of this and that's okay too. Just as there are different versions of a single event, a book can be used by different people in different ways!

I have consciously stayed away from too many conscious judgements of 'good' and 'bad' since I believe we must benefit from the past rather than be burdened by it. So, in every personality discussed in the book, I have found something we can learn, either to do or otherwise.

I hope the book helps you see history as being relevant for you to navigate through your life and career and helps you find answers for your personal quest. At the very least, I hope it gives you hours of reading pleasure.

Accounts of the West

MALIK AMBAR

> *Malik Ambar (1548–1626) was originally from Ethiopia who attained fame and fortune in the Deccan. Starting life as a slave, he went on to become a soldier, then commanded an army, established a kingdom and remained undefeated by the Mughals due to his innovative guerrilla warfare tactics. The city he founded—Aurangabad—was a marvel of town planning and gives us a glimpse of his administrative skills. Malik Ambar is a footnote in the history of India but is worthy of deeper study for his sheer resourcefulness, ingenuity and above all, his survival skills.*

Arrival in India

Many rulers in India preferred to trust soldiers who were slaves, in preference to their own nobles. To buy slaves, they preferred Africa—a place as far away from India as possible. These slaves were treated as property. Most of them were loyal to their masters who protected them and ranked loyalty to their master above the whispers of jealous nobles who wanted them to fight against their masters. The relationship between the slave and the master was very clear. The slave was always a property, never an heir, and his only task was to fight for his master.

Such slaves purchased from Africa were called 'Habshi', from the word, 'Abyssinia' (which was the old name of Ethiopia), the most popular supply point. Born around 1548 in the Oromo tribe, Ambar was purchased for twenty gold ducats by an Arab. He passed through other owners and finally came to one who converted him to Islam, brought him to India and sold him to the Peshwa or chief minister of the Ahmednagar Sultanate. Malik was in his twenties then. His new owner (a freed slave himself) died soon after and Malik Ambar was given his freedom by his widow.

From then, for the next twenty years, he was a mercenary with a small, loyal army. He found steady employment with the Adil Shah rulers of Bijapur. It was in the early 1590s when the Mughals invaded Ahmednagar that Malik Ambar's star began to ascend. Starting with about 150 men under his command, after the fall of Ahmednagar to the Mughals, he began leading his men as an independent mercenary cohort. Within a year of the fall of the city, he commanded 3,000 warriors. By 1600, it was almost 7,000, including Marathas and Dakhnis (local Muslims).

This astonishing rise in the strength of his army was because of his own charismatic personality that inspired trust. In that time, for an Ethiopian to command trust in India when caste and religion where important markers of identity are noteworthy. The Deccan was far more international then—it had people from Iran, Turkey and Afghanistan jostling for power with the Marathas. To make a mark among all these people vying with each other for control is commendable. Ambar was able to get financial support from other kingdoms by promising to fight against their common enemy, the Mughals. He was able to deliver on this promise and that created trust with the kings who funded him, the soldiers who fought for him and the people who accepted his rule.

The de-facto ruler of Ahmednagar

Malik Ambar was also careful to fight not for himself but for his master. As an outsider in India promoting himself as king at the beginning of his independent journey would have ruffled too many feathers. He acted cautiously and used his victories to build his reputation. When the Mughals deposed the young Nizam Shahi sultan of Ahmednagar, Malik Ambar found another relative and declared him Murtaza Nizam Shah II. From his headquarters of Parenda, he declared war on the Mughals in the name of the new king and stated that the Mughals were unlawfully meddling in the affairs of Ahmednagar.

Ambar's guerrilla warfare, called 'bhargi-giri', managed to exhaust the Mughals who agreed to peace. They recognised the new boundaries of Ahmednagar. By now, in common parlance, it was known as 'Ambar's land'. The Nizam Shah king was still on the throne but everyone knew Malik Ambar was the real power.

His power did not go uncontested. To consolidate his position, he had his daughter married to the Nizam, Murtaza II. However, the Nizam's more senior Persian wife had an argument with her and the Nizam also tried asserting himself. Malik Ambar had both the Persian wife as well as Murtaza II killed in 1610. He then elevated Murtaza's young son as king (Burhan III).

His skill as a builder—the new capital city

While Ambar would formally greet his new king twice a week, thereby asserting the king's supremacy, in reality, he called the shots. At some point, Ambar decided his new king needed a grand new capital. We don't know if Burhan III really wanted it but Ambar certainly did, and in 1610, he established a new capital, Khirki. It was a testament to his remarkable vision for urban planning. It had fifty-four sectors and at its height, a population of 200,000. This was all the more noteworthy since the region is very dry, drought-prone and starved of water. This issue was resolved with a complex water storage and irrigation system. He named some of the sectors after Maratha generals, as the Marathas were an invaluable asset to him—Paraspura, Vithapura, Khelpura to name a few. At this point his army comprised around 10,000 Habshis and 40,000 Dakhnis (mostly Marathas).

Unconquered by the Mughals

Even as Khirki was flourishing, Ambar continued to fight the Mughals, who were ever eager to expand their kingdom southwards. In 1616, he faced a very serious setback. The Maratha forces switched loyalties to the Mughals and the Mughal army led by Prince Khurram (later Shah Jahan) defeated the Nizam Shahis. Ambar lost Khirki, which was largely destroyed by the Maratha army. But Ambar was smart; he knew he had to accept defeat and even at this time, he managed to keep a small part of the kingdom still in the name of the Nizam Shahi dynasty. He now had to wait patiently for his time to win back his city of Khirki and the kingdom.

The next year, however, his ally Ibrahim Adil Shah II of Bijaipur switched sides, and allied with the Mughals when Prince Khurram offered to share the Nizam Shahi territories with Adil Shah of Bijaipur. Ambar had a few minor wars but the increasing pressure of other local kings allying with the Mughals meant Ambar had to fight hard and win decisively. The local kings had quickly forgotten an important lesson from their own history. They had captured the Vijayanagar empire because they were united. Now they were vying with each other to ingratiate themselves to the Mughals rather than working with Ambar on how they could be independent.

In 1624, Ambar attacked Bijapur, the capital of Ibrahim Adil Shah II. Before the Bijapuris could retaliate, he retreated to his own territory. He wanted to fight in his zone of comfort. It was a shrewd move. He had the area flooded into a slush. The Mughal army marched in support of their ally Adil Shah II. The organised (and, therefore, inflexible) army could not fight Ambar's bhargi-giri warfare. Every night, they were mercilessly attacked by Ambar's army. Ambar won the battle of Bhataudi. From 1624 till his death in 1626, he continued to expand his territory, reconquer lost ones, rebuilt Khirki and remained undefeated by the Mughals.

Over the years, there had been many attempts on Ambar's life, none of them successful. Ambar had been a thorn in the side of Jahangir for almost his entire reign. Jahangir even commissioned a painting of him shooting an arrow into the severed head of Malik Ambar. Though purely symbolic, he had hoped all his life to have Ambar killed. He was thwarted in the end when Ambar, almost eighty, died in 1626, of old age.

After Malik Ambar

After the death of Malik Ambar, his son Fateh Khan kept up the resistance but he did not have the leadership qualities of his father. The Mughals were soon able to occupy the kingdom. Other descendants of Malik Ambar were propped up by nobles but they did not have the leadership ability to outwit the Mughals. When Bijapur and Golconda were fully conquered by the Mughals, all the territory of Malik Ambar was also incorporated into the Mughal empire.

Life lessons

Personal resilience

Malik Ambar came to India as an Ethiopian slave and died the ruler of an independent kingdom with a loyal army unconquered by the most powerful army of that time—the Mughals. As a foreigner in this land, it must have been difficult for him and he clearly possessed enormous courage and resilience to overcome all hurdles and focus on his ascent to the top.

Guerrilla warfare tactics

Today, it is vital for an organisation to understand the geography of its sites of production and those of its customers. 'What to make?' and 'where to sell?' are the two basic questions of any business and these are both connected to geography. Proximity to natural resources and understanding the climate of the customer's land are small but vital details. For example, thermal power companies are often located near water bodies since they require a lot of water to cool their plants. An automobile company discovered the importance of understanding local geography when it designed low floor buses that worked well for Europe but not for the monsoon flooded roads of Asia!

Malik knew his geography well and turned it to his advantage. One of his early biographers compared him to a deciduous tree in the Deccan—it knows when to grow leaves and when to drop them and conserve its resources. Ambar knew when to fight a battle, when to win through trickery and when to be quiet and wait.

Added to this was his flexible, nimble approach and the larger but more procedure-driven, inflexible Mughal army was defeated. Without Malik Ambar and his military prowess, the Nizam Shahi resistance would have ended years before it did. Due to Malik Ambar, both Akbar as well as Jahangir were unable to confidently believe that the Nizam Shahis were subdued and that Ahmednagar was a Mughal province. Bijapur and Golconda held out as well, but with marriage alliances and gifts, that weakened them severely. The Nizam Shahis, in the time of Malik Ambar, held out bravely, with their heads held high.

Malik Ambar is to be credited with refining guerrilla warfare in the Deccan. The whole strategy of strategised attacks was not too popular before his time, and it is believed that he learnt it in the highlands of Ethiopia in his childhood perhaps when he was hunting animals by stalking them and attacking them when they least expected it. The Mughals called it bhargi-giri and this style of ambush rather than direct fighting influenced him.

Once he had taken over control of the Nizam Shahi territory, Ambar fine-tuned the art of guerrilla warfare, using it over and over again in the arid rocky Deccan, where an army could escape into the hills and launch surprise attacks. His tactics were later adapted by the Marathas.

One of Ambar's closest aides was a man called Maloji. Maloji was a cavalryman, who later became the Jaghirdar of Pune under Malik Ambar. He died in 1606, and his young son, Shahaji, inherited the Jagir. Shahji was very close to Malik Ambar, and was the chief general at the 1624 Battle of Bhataudi, where a vastly outnumbered Ahmednagar army defeated Jahangir and his men, by opening up a nearby dam, and flooding the Mughal camp. Bhargi-giri came into play here, as knowledge of local landscape meant the Ahmednagar army knew how best to defeat the vastly superior Mughals without using or losing too many men.

Shahaji was the father of Shivaji, who inherited his guerrilla tactics from Malik Ambar, through his father. In Shivaji, Jahangir's grandson Aurangzeb found an adversary who would prove to be as troublesome to his empire as Malik Ambar was to his grandfather's, and later found a kingdom that would be a thorn in Aurangzeb's side.

Administrative expertise

Malik Ambar was not just a courageous and innovative soldier. He knew how to consolidate as well. Once his kingdom was relatively safe, he built his capital with much thought and precision.

The city of Khirki, or Khadki, was built to withstand the Mughal onslaught. It was built as a multicultural hub, with mosques, temples and even a church. To ensure its survival, and the survival of its people, Ambar devised a water supply system, something much-needed in the dry rocky Deccan. This was a complex long-lasting system designed to remain intact even when the city was under siege. This water system was later improved by Aurangzeb.

Khirki was taken by the Mughals in 1616, but Ambar took it back subsequently. In the time of Shah Jahan, his young son conquered the city and renamed it after himself—Aurangabad (from Aurangzeb).

The business connection

Life seems to have dealt Ambar many bad cards but he was able to convert each one of them into an opportunity. It seems that fortune favours those who respond quickly and decisively to change. People like Ambar are quick thinkers who capitalise on opportunities. They were not born to rule. They improvised, came up winners and then manoeuvred to stay in their place. Such people cannot think in terms of a legacy when they are forever caught up in survival. He spent all his time playing the game, and did not plan his succession. While we can learn survival skills from him, we also need to be cautious of something he was not cautious about—planning for the future. Perhaps Malik could have chosen a meritorious soldier to succeed him or trained a family member.

An Indian success story comparable is that of Dhirubai Ambani who, through his daring risk-taking ability and complex survival strategies, was able to rise from the son of a poor school teacher to build one of India's largest companies. In his growth story, he faced many obstacles, significant among them rights issue with the Bombay Stock Exchange, but he never let that hamper him and instead worked his way through to resolve it to make the Reliance brand one of the largest and strongest. In the Ambani case as well, succession between his two sons was not easy and relations have not been the most harmonious.

However, amongst all the changes of guards and brands, there was a visible tapestry of continuity, the very thing lacking in the legacy of Malik Ambar. The diversification also demonstrates the other missing pieces from the legacy of Malik Ambar—constantly seeing change and responding to it quickly and decisively.

Conclusion

Today, we have many (but not as many as we should) people from the poorest, neglected parts of our society rising up and making a name for themselves. With far greater access to education, health and opportunities than in the past, it is still difficult for them and they persevere through grit, determination and persistence. If the obstacles are many today, imagine how many more there would have been 500 years ago. Add to this Ambar's origins as a foreigner and you realise how complicated his task was.

For this and the subsequent essays, consider reflecting on what other lessons you can learn from the leader.

Further Reading

Manu S. Pillai, *Rebel Sultans: the Deccan from Khilji to Shivaji*, (Juggernaut, 2018)

Jonathan Gil Harris, *The First Firangis: Remarkable Stories of Heroes, Healers, Charlatans, Courtesans & Other Foreigners Who Became Indian* (Aleph Book Company, 2016)

Parvati Sharma, *Jahangir: An Intimate Portrait of a Great Mughal* (Juggernaut, 2018)

THE DECCAN SULTANATES

The word 'Deccan' comes from the Sanskrit word 'dakshina', which means south. It refers to the land south of the Vindhya mountains, which is situated between the east and west coast. Although geographically it stands for the entire southern India, in the study of history, it is generally considered to be the area of present-day Maharashtra, northern Karnataka and northern Andhra Pradesh.

This region was a part of the Bahamani kingdom that had conquered this area from the Delhi Sultans. Ala-ud-Din Bahman Shah established the kingdom in 1347. By 1518, the kingdom was in serious decline. Successive rulers had become more and more reliant on their vizier or prime minister and had neglected to keep a personal touch with their army. They were also dependent on the support of powerful local military commanders and landowners. The kingdom then broke up into five smaller kingdoms: Ahmednagar, Golconda (Hyderabad), Bidar, Berar and Bijapur. The former governors of these provinces now styled themselves sultans. While they constantly quarrelled among themselves initially, in course of time, they came together to defeat the mighty Vijayanagar empire in 1565.

Differences and conflicts between the Deccan states

There were various differences between the five states. The seat of power was with Bidar at first, as that was where the Bahmani emperors had ruled from. Bijapur and Golconda were economically better off. Bijapur controlled the ports that brought in trade from Arabia and Persia to the Deccan. Golconda was renowned for its wealth and its mines were well known. This meant that each of the kingdoms followed a different trajectory.

In addition, there were religious differences. While the other four sultanates followed Sunni Islam, Bijapur's state religion fluctuated between Sunni and Shia Islam.

Even in their origins there were differences. The sultans of Golconda and Bijapur had Persian and Turkish ancestry, while the other three rulers were of local origin.

Though the states all fought each other from time to time, ranging from occasional raids into each other's territories, all the way to actual battles, there was a need felt, right from the formation, that only by ensuring the survival of the other states would they survive.

Soon after their formation, Bijapur declared Shia Islam to be its state religion, in order to curry favour with Persia. This did not go down well with three other kingdoms, who banded together to bring down Bijapur. However, the Imad Shah of Berar prevented this by explaining to the others that in order for all of them to survive, they needed to stand together and attacking Bijapur would be a dangerous precedent to set, leading to chaos among the states. Chastened, the kingdoms backed off and continued in relative harmony.

Relationship with Vijayanagar

It was in the interest of the Vijayanagar kings that the Deccan states not unite and attack Vijayanagar and so they constantly played one state against another.

When Krishnadeva Raya died in 1530, his brother Achyutha Deva Raya ruled for a brief period. After his death in 1542, however, an erstwhile general from the Deccan, who had married into the Vijayanagar family, Ramaraya, seized power, and declared himself regent to the young king, Achyutha Deva Raya's son.

Ramaraya looked to play the Deccan states, never the strongest of allies, with constant internal feuding, against one another, and thereby expand Vijayanagar northward. In 1543, he prompted the Nizam Shah against the Adil Shah, and helped him capture territories. Later, he encouraged a rebellion in Golconda. In 1558, he allied with the Adil Shah against the Nizam Shah. With the might of Vijayanagar's army behind him, Ali Adil Shah besieged Ahmednagar, and the Nizam Shah had to flee. In 1561, Ahmednagar sued for peace. However, the conditions put down were humiliating and played a role in the shape of things to come as Ramaraya's ploy of using his rivals' differences to his advantage and turning them against each other backfired very badly.

The Qutb Shah, who had allied with Vijayanagar and the Adil Shah in the war against Ahmednagar initially, was not too happy with the way it had gone, and had withdrawn half way. He now made overtures to the Nizam Shah. A marital alliance between them sealed their friendship.

Following this, the Adil Shah and Vijayanagar invaded Ahmednagar again and this time, Ramaraya did not just plunder the countryside but destroyed mosques and killed and injured civilians. He even raided his ally the Adil Shah's territories.

As it turned out, the sultanates eventually came to the conclusion that their future could be secured only if they united against Vijayanagar. In December 1564, four of the five sultanates (Bidar did not join) marched across the Krishna into Vijayanagar territory.

The battle between the two armies took place on 3 January 1565. The battle was won with the death of Ramaraya.

A few days later, the Deccan armies entered the city. For months afterward, they plundered, looted and destroyed.

Enormous wealth was plundered, and the city of Hampi would never go back to the magnificent state it had been in ever again. Today, the ruins of Hampi give us an indication of the splendour of this cosmopolitan capital.

The Deccan states after the defeat of Vijayanagar

After the fall of Vijayanagar, the allies returned to their respective kingdoms. Within a few years, they went back to fighting each other. In 1574, Ahmednagar overran Berar. Bidar was swallowed up by Bijapur later in 1619. Around this time, the Mughal empire also began expanding southwards. This time round, there was no attempt to unite to resist the common enemy. Owing to Malik Ambar's genius, Ahmednagar resisted, but post Ambar's death, it too fell.

Business lessons from the Deccan States

To ensure mutual survival, the states initially put aside their differences. To take down a common enemy, the states later entered into an alliance and put aside their differences a second time. This ensured their survival. However, they fell in the end, unable to put aside their differences when the Mughals came.

It also underlines the truth in the dictum 'united we stand, divided we fall'. From an organisational point of view, that would be bringing locations, departments and regions together. The methods could vary. But constant communication, meetings, consensus-driven decision-making, frequent job rotation, rewards and recognition systems that incentivise working together and effective feedback mechanisms are some ideas to achieve this.

Personal touch

I am reminded of a senior sales head of a large auto company. A 'let's go and attack the market today' kind of person who was bubbling with energy, he was never one to see the customer market as a battlefield, which was the usual terminology I heard from sales teams. When he got his team together in goal-setting off-sites, he would be just as aggressive in setting goals, exhorting his team to do better, but the terminology never borrowed from battle scenarios and did not invoke 'let's kill the competition' kind of dialogue. He treated the competition with respect, listened intently from the field about what they did differently and, most importantly, about how they added value to the client. The approach was competitive, but the emotional connect was built not from loss framing but from finding out how to add value to the client rather than destroy competition.

I asked him once why he did not use the battle and victory analogy so beloved of marketing heads. He said, 'Look, there is always going to be a competitor whether I like it or not, so might as well turn it to my advantage and learn from them because you can never defeat all competition and even if you did, it won't last forever because our industry is so cyclical. We may as well divert the battle-fighting energy to build a deeper emotional connect with the customer and add more value to them.' I am sure he lost a few battles because of this but I am also sure he mostly won the war!

Further Reading

Rajmohan Gandhi, *Modern South India: A History from the 17th Century to Our Times* (Aleph Book Company, 2018)

Manu S. Pillai, *Rebel Sultans: the Deccan from Khilji to Shivaji* (Juggernaut, 2018)

Robert Sewell et al. *A Forgotten Empire (Vijayanagar): A Contribution to the History of India* (Asian Educational Services, 2004)

CHHATRAPATI SHIVAJI

Today, Chhatrapati Shivaji (1630–1680) is considered a national hero and is arguably the most talked about figure from Maharashtra. Stories of his life and his achievements form an integral part of the upbringing and identity of Maharashtrians, passed on from generation to generation through popular plays and ballads. Shivaji's statues and monuments are found almost in every village, town and city in Maharashtra as well as in different places across India. Other commemorations include roads named after him, the Indian Navy's ship the INS Shivaji, postage stamps, and the names of the airport and the main railway terminus in Mumbai. In addition, a proposal to build a statue of Shivaji near Mumbai was also approved in 2016. It is expected to be 210 metres tall, making it the world's biggest statue when it is completed.

Clearly, a larger-than-life figure, Shivaji's life and career are worthy of examination for the many things it could teach us.

Early years and influences

Shivaji was born to Jijabai and Shahaji, the chieftain of Pune and Supe districts in the court of the Nizam Shah of Ahmednagar, in 1630, and belonged to the Bhonsle clan of the Marathas. He was born in the hill-fort of Shivneri in today's Pune district in Maharashtra.

In the early seventeenth century, the Deccan region was split between the Sultanates of Bijapur, Golconda and Ahmednagar and the Mughals who under Shah Jahan controlled regions to the north of the Sahyadris. With the fall of the Vijayanagara empire in the mid-seventeenth century, the Bijapur Sultanate took over their possessions in the areas of present-day north Karnataka and Maharashtra.

When Shivaji was born, Shahaji Bhonsle was serving under the Bijapur Sultanate. In 1639, Shahaji was stationed in today's Bangalore and he brought with him, Shivaji, his elder brother Sambhaji and step-brother Ekoji who were then formally educated and trained.

Jijabai had a huge moral, religious and spiritual influence on Shivaji in his early years. She instilled in him the qualities of faith, humanity, equality and spirituality through her teaching of the Ramayana and Mahabharata. In addition to Jijabai, Dadoji Kondadev was responsible for Shivaji's all-round development in the areas of warfare and social and political administration, providing valuable insights and developing his creative decision-making skills in the face of adversities. The seeds of developing an able leader were sown early by both these individuals.

The early experiences of his childhood went a long way. The right mentorship was critical in developing Shivaji as a leader and also as a human being. Later, owing to his early training, he ensured that they would reflect in his social, political, administrative and military systems.

The geography of the Mawal region of Maharashtra has had an influence in moulding the character and history of its people. The region is encircled on two sides by the mountain ranges of the Sahyadri, running from north to south, and the Satpura and the Vindhyas, running from east to west. Shivaji travelled the countryside and the inaccessible regions of the Sahyadris with his friends such as Tanaji Malusare and Baji Prabhu Deshpande, gaining familiarity with the terrain that would prove useful in his military conquests.

It was in these journeys that he articulated his concept of Swaraj. At the young age of fifteen, Shivaji expressed his idea of Swaraj, a state not dictated to by the Sultanates. He was keen on building his own independent administrative systems with each and every one of his ministers, officers as well as peasants being in perfect sync with his larger goal of Swaraj.

It was during these travels that he developed an effective network of communication when he came into contact with local farmers, peasants and civilians of the Maratha region. Shivaji also realised the importance of a strong intelligence network. The rugged and unproductive soil of the land, its scanty rainfall and precarious water conditions and its meagre agricultural resources had helped people develop the virtues of self-reliance, endurance, courage, perseverance and a sense of social equality.

His travels had also taught Shivaji that hill-forts in the Mawal region were often neglected by the Sultanate rulers and were suitable for resisting potential enemies. These forts, in addition to establishing and sustaining the empire, were critical for the security and surveillance of the region.

However, with a military strength of a few thousand loyal soldiers, he knew he was no match for the Sultanates in a direct battle yet. He, therefore, began cautiously. From 1645, he started conquering local regions through his skills of guile and persuasion. First, he bribed Inayat Khan, the local commander and conquered Torna fort without a contest. This was followed by the capture of Rajgad fort, Chakan fort (near Pune), Kondana (later called Sinhagad) and Purandar in the vicinity of Pune. Outwardly, he continued to profess his loyalty to the Bijapur Sultanate even as he prepared for Swaraj.

In 1648, understanding the gravity of the situation, Sultan

Adil Shah of Bijapur ordered the arrest of Shahaji. Then he ordered Fateh Khan to tackle Shivaji in Kondana and also Farhad Khan to annex Bangalore from Shivaji's brother, Sambhaji. The in-depth knowledge of the terrain helped Shivaji rout Fateh Khan's forces and they had to retreat to Bijapur. Shahaji's arrest though put restrictions on Shivaji's activities. He was now in a terrible dilemma: neither could he surrender and sacrifice his hopes of Swaraj nor could he leave his father in danger of torture. However, in a Machiavellian move, Shivaji displayed tactful diplomacy and a servile attitude towards the Mughal emperor, invoking his patronage. This indirectly put pressure on the Bijapur Sultanate and they sought reconciliation. Shahaji was released conditionally and given back his jagirs. Also, Shahaji on his part instructed Shivaji to return the Kondana fort.

Shivaji decided to consolidate his territories and focus more on organising his administrative structure, restructuring his military forces and looking after the welfare of his people by engaging in populist measures. This showed Shivaji to be a very prudent and pragmatic leader who was willing to bide time for his conquests.

Eventually, Shivaji went on to carve out his own kingdom against all odds and lay the ground for the powerful Maratha forces who dominated much of the subcontinent in the eighteenth century.

Life lessons

Using the land to his advantage

Being outnumbered by the Sultanate and Mughal forces in all his battles against them, Shivaji understood very early that guerrilla warfare was the best way to tackle his opponents. His attacks were often based on the principles of a sudden raid with minimum loss and maximum damage to the enemy. His soldiers, many of them from the local tribes of the region, were accustomed to the terrain unlike his adversaries and the element of surprise coupled with tenacious execution made them a force to reckon with. He had to often rely on quick thinking and be flexible to adapt to the surrounding environment. Shivaji developed and devised a technique of defence and offence through the construction of a series of forts in the high hills to supplement his guerrilla warfare.

Shivaji's army was a rapidly moving light cavalry with its strengths being speed of attack, operational mobility, and an ability to strike at unexpected places and time. It could cut off supply lines to enemies in an instant. The force was disciplined with good endurance and survival skills and often fought the enemy at a place and time of its choice. This helped Shivaji win several decisive victories such as the ones in the Konkan, Pune, Ahmednagar and the major one in Surat over formidable adversaries.

The agility of Shivaji's army came from its mastery of the geographic terrain and the ability to rethink and recalibrate strategy swiftly as the situations changed. Contrast this with the larger and, therefore, less nimble Mughal army. The highly organised and large Mughal army was unable to swiftly march through dense forests and tackle the mountainous terrain. Both Shivaji and the Ahoms exploited this weakness, since they chose to play to their strengths rather than focus on the strength of the opponent.

However, his guerrilla strategies did have its disadvantages. His forces often found it difficult to win enemy territories through storming and sapping methods of warfare. They also lacked provisioning facilities during sieges and during battles and were often forced to live off the land. This was observed in the Marathas ceding defeat in the battles of Panhala and Purandar. Also, they found it difficult to establish continuous rule over a territory. Shivaji could not provide protection to cultivation and trade, which would have made the area prosper financially.

His ability to connect and build relationships

When Shivaji travelled in his younger days, he had managed to develop an effective way of communicating with the local farmers, peasants and civilians of the region.

In Shivaji, they saw a leader who would be responsive to their situation. His words, spoken from the heart, were often a reflection of their pain and agony and how he could help alleviate their suffering. They were impressed by Shivaji's qualities of honesty, truthfulness and trust.

This can be observed in an incident that took place during the campaign to capture Kondana Fort. Tanaji Malusare, one of his army generals and a trusted friend, insisted on finishing the campaign before conducting his son's marriage. Unfortunately, he was killed in battle. Upon hearing the news of the death of his most beloved friend and commander, Shivaji remarked: '*Gad ala pan Sinha gela.*' (We have gained the fort, but lost a lion.). He went on to rename Kondhana fort as Sinhagad (Lion Fort) and later conducted the wedding of Tanaji's son as if it were his own son's wedding.

His speed and his street-smart tactics

Shivaji also realised the importance of a strong intelligence network. He and his generals were ably supported by a well-connected set of spies who provided vital information at critical times.

Shivaji was a mastermind in surprise moves that were often very innovative as well. He used this for his clashes with the Bijapur Sultanate and Mughals. Shivaji's first confrontation with the Mughals was in March 1657. Bahadur Khan was deceived by Shivaji in the battle of Ahmednagar. He was misled into believing that Shivaji wished to submit a petition seeking peace negotiations with the emperor. With a well-planned and well-executed stealth attack, Shivaji's forces raided the Mughal barracks and made away with battle-hardened Arabian horses and plenty of loot.

Aurangzeb responded to these raids by sending Nasiri Khan, who defeated the forces of Shivaji at Ahmednagar. However, Aurangzeb's countermeasures against Shivaji were interrupted by his battle of succession with his brothers for the Mughal throne following the illness and death of Shah Jahan.

In 1659, the veteran general of the Bijapur Sultanate, Afzal Khan, fell into Shivaji's trap and paid with his life, which led to a complete rout of the Bijapur forces in the Battle of Pratapgarh. This encounter was the final nail in the Bijapur Sultanate's coffin and became the stuff of Maratha legend. This encounter also showed that Shivaji was never intimidated by the enemy's size and often thought a few steps ahead of them.

Having defeated the Bijapur forces, Shivaji's army then marched towards the Konkan and Kolhapur, seizing Panhala fort. With these victories, the Marathas under Shivaji transformed into a strong military force, gaining soldiers, artillery, war-horses, forts and territory. Shivaji also realised the importance of naval power very early and built a fleet of small and speedy ships. This showed his foresight to equip his military with new innovative trends and technologies.

In 1660, the Bijapur Sultanate entered into an alliance with the Mughals, now headed by Aurangzeb who had won the battle for succession over his brothers. Their intention was to tackle the wily and audacious Shivaji. Their joint forces were also bolstered by the advanced artillery they had purchased from the British. The Mughals under Aurangzeb's uncle Shaishta Khan were to attack Panhala from the north, while the Bijapur forces under Siddi Jauhar blocked the southern borders. Shivaji, anticipating this, had entered into a clandestine agreement with the administrator of Vishalgad to ensure his safety. During the siege of Panhala, Shivaji decided to cater to the ego of Siddi Jauhar. He was lured into a false sense of complacency by Shivaji's promise of surrendering the fort. One of Shivaji's followers who resembled him and a few hundred soldiers were sent to Siddi Jauhar. This bought Shivaji enough time to retreat to Vishalgad fort. The Marathas suffered losses, including the death of Shivaji's close comrade, Baji Prabhu Deshpande, but yet again, Shivaji's swift move enabled him to escape a calamitous situation.

Meanwhile, Shaishta Khan was able to seize forts and territories lost to the Maratha rebels and he had established his base at Shivaji's Palace at Lal Mahal. In 1663, in a daring midnight raid on the palace, led by Shivaji himself, the Marathas killed Shaishta Khan's son, while Shivaji himself maimed Shaishta Khan. Also, in response to the Mughal attacks on the Pune region, Shivaji ransacked Surat, the wealthy trading hub of the Mughals.

The twin attacks enraged Aurangzeb and he now sent his Rajput general, Raja Jai Singh, who had served the Mughals from the time of Shah Jahan. The Mughal cavalry devastated the countryside and also recaptured many of the forts. In addition to wins on the field, many of Shivaji's commanders and cavalrymen defected to the Mughals. The Mughals also succeeded in conquering the fort of Purandar. Foreseeing defeat, Shivaji agreed to a truce after his safety was assured by Raja Jai Singh. He signed the Treaty of Purandar in 1665 by agreeing to give up twenty-three of his forts, paying compensation and also helping the Mughals to conquer lost territories in the Deccan as one of their military units.

As a follow-up to this treaty, Shivaji and his son Sambhaji were summoned by Aurangzeb to Agra. Although Shivaji saw himself as a regional king, in the eyes of Aurangzeb he was just a successful zamindar-rebel from the Deccan and he treated him accordingly. This irritated Shivaji. Later, Shivaji and his son were placed under house arrest due to his apparent misbehaviour and refusal to help the Mughals in their conflict with the Afghans. His goods and jewels were confiscated. When all hope of a rapprochement between Aurangzeb and Shivaji failed, Shivaji managed to escape quietly after negotiating a loan with a patron in Aurangzeb's court.

Knowing when to strike back

Back in the Deccan, the following three years (1665–68) were ones of diplomatic peace with the Mughals. Shivaji offered his submission to Aurangzeb recognising that a Mughal army of the nature of Jai Singh's could once again overwhelm his forces. Until 1669, Shivaji's campaigns were minor, centred on consolidating his territories.

The peace broke down once again in 1669–70. Shivaji now launched rapid attacks to recover his lost forts. Within six months, Shivaji's forces had captured Sinhagad, Purandar, Rohida, Lohgad and Mahuli. In 1670, Shivaji attacked Surat for the second time. Although the British and Dutch factories were able to repel his attack, he managed to ransack the city itself once again, obtaining much booty. This was followed by raids on British factories in Bombay, as they had refused to sell him war material and also as revenge for the British helping the Mughals with artillery during the Siege of Panhala earlier.

In subsequent years, he raided Khandesh, Karwar, Kohlapur, Berar and Baglan, which gave him control over trade routes. He then recaptured territories to the south of Pune, including Nashik, Panhala and the Konkan coast. Throughout this period, Shivaji was fortunate that the Mughals were occupied with their battles in the north and the north-western frontier. In 1674, after much debate over his lineage and ancestry, Shivaji was crowned Chhatrapati. From 1674 to his death in 1680, Shivaji was mainly involved in campaigns in the south. He invaded Golconda first and then went on to capture Gingee in today's Tamil Nadu where he both fought and negotiated with Ekoji (his half-brother) and took the major fort of Vellore. Shivaji proposed dividing the polity with his younger son, Rajaram, getting the heartland areas of Maharashtra and his older son, Sambhaji, getting the new conquests in the south. These problems remained unresolved at the time of Shivaji's death.

After a lingering illness of two years, Shivaji died in 1680. He left a state with a full treasury, more than a hundred forts in the Western Ghats and territories in the Deccan, Konkan and in southern India. Overall, Shivaji left the Marathas in a good state who were at odds with the Mughals but well able to defend themselves. Although Aurangzeb was successful in overthrowing the Deccan Sultanates, he was unable to subdue the Marathas despite spending twenty-seven years in the Deccan after Shivaji's death.

Operational and administrative rigour

Shivaji had the dual quality of being both a strategic warrior as well as a shrewd administrator. His sound administration coupled with his own courage and charisma helped him retain conquered territory. Shivaji ensured that the vision, mission, objectives of all his organisational systems were crafted to align with his idea of Swaraj. He strongly believed that administrative tasks could not be treated as mundane and that experts had to be employed to provide a complete view of organisational management from top to bottom. It was a mandate for people in these systems to be in sync with the larger identified goals. These advisors were open-minded and honest decision makers who allowed the king to take the right decisions and move closer towards his idea of self-governance. The Maratha administration can be studied under three heads—central administration, revenue administration and military administration.

His central administration was largely inspired by the Deccan Sultanate administration and was focused on catering to the well-being of his subjects. Shivaji was an able thinker and believed in sound systems and processes in provincial administration. He introduced the concept of the 'ashthapradhan' council (a cabinet of eight ministers), along with clearly defined roles and responsibilities. Appointment to this council was based on efficiency. He also focused on grassroots-level administration and laid a good foundation of processes and systems right across the hierarchy. The procedures were made independent to ensure they worked well even in his absence. He also ensured that none of the positions were permanent or hereditary. Each minister was further assisted by a group of clerks to ensure smooth functioning. Shivaji divided his entire territory into provinces, each under a viceroy. He further divided the provinces into 'prants' (districts) and then 'pargana' or 'tarafs' (group of villages or sub-division of a district). The lowest unit was the village, which was headed by a Patil.

Recruitment into his administrative services was largely based on merit and subject to efficient performance. A method of referral was followed, which ensured that a background check to ensure integrity of the candidate was an important prerequisite. The trustee played the main role in selecting the right person for the right job and a complete check was made on the skill set, character and loyalty of the person. This ensured mapping of the right person for the right job based on their skill set and core competencies.

Also, Shivaji believed in integrating all communities into his administrative systems. The farmers and malis (gardeners) were in-charge of ensuring food supply while other groups catered to the requirements of the military and the administrative systems. He also did not significantly attack the power of the ruling elite families of Maharashtra, and they were largely left in peace, as it would have been impossible for him to govern without their support. His policies ensured that they would be integrated into the fold.

Shivaji developed two systems of recruitment for the army—one on a full-time salaried basis and another on a contractual basis. When there was no war, the ones recruited to the army on a temporary basis would work in the fields. Thus, there was never a shortage of manpower.

He also did not follow the jagirdar system, an existing system under the Islamic Sultanates where the landlords were allotted jagirs (districts) to govern and collect land revenues for the services rendered by them to the Mughal Empire. The jagirdar system was a major part of revenue for the Deccan Sultanates. Shivaji preferred the ryotwari system in which the state had direct contact with peasants. In this system, the cultivators were asked to pay a percentage of their assessed produce to the state. The farmers had the option to pay land revenue in cash or kind and could pay the revenue in instalments. The accounts of the revenue officers were thoroughly checked. The officers were paid in cash from the state treasury.

Shivaji was also known for his liberal and tolerant religious policy. He was inclusive and respected all cultures, communities and religions. Being a pluralist, he was able to gain support across communities. While Hindus were able to follow their religion freely, he allowed Muslims to practise without harassment and also supported them with endowments. When Aurangzeb issued a fresh order imposing the jizya tax (a tax imposed on non-Muslims) on the Hindu populace, Shivaji wrote a strong letter of protest stating: 'God is the Lord of all men and not of the Muhammadans only. Islam and Hinduism are only different pigments used by the divine painter to picture the human species.' He had many

Muslims serving him in his military and had no qualms about allying with the Islamic Sultanates for his political gain. Moreover, he never allied with the other Hindu powers, such as the Rajputs, who were rebelling against the Mughals, as the Marathas were interested in becoming a hegemony. Also, the Rajputs were a divided lot with many rulers forming close relationships with the Mughal emperors and serving them in different capacities.

The business connection

All entrepreneurs and business leaders are survivors like Shivaji. Working with several institutional stakeholders, each having several policies and rules and the rapid change in market share, the constant need to balance various stakeholders are all potential deal-breakers for anyone looking for success.

Shivaji's creative ways to stay one step ahead of competition and his use of the knowledge of the land (in the business case it would be the geography of the market and the local environment) are all lessons worth reflecting upon.

Shivaji was, for much of his life, a subordinate to the Mughals, yet that did not serve as an excuse or prevent him from pursuing his own ambitions. He probably found his energy through internal conviction and spirituality. All leaders too need to find their own ways of harnessing what gives them energy to convert adversity to opportunity.

Personal touch

Shivaji today is an icon for most Indians. Many strive to appropriate his legacy as their own and it is impossible to write anything about him that takes away from his greatness! In a way, he has almost attained divine status.

Shivaji was a brilliant tactician and a survivor. Tactics in war alone cannot create a legacy. One also has to be able to persuade others to be accepted as a leader. Heredity alone is also not enough. In Shivaji's case, he seems to have set a powerful example by his own speech and behaviour. Clearly, the stories he heard as a child imbued him with strong values. Translating them into speech and behaviour towards the poor farmer and the powerful military general seems to have been a key ingredient of his charisma.

Human beings tend to do what leaders do rather than do what leaders say. In my long consulting career, leaders I have seen who were seen as inspirational by their teams did small things that showcased their sincerity, commitment and their ability to walk the talk. It may have been replying to emails and calls promptly, not keeping others waiting, even switching off the lights as they left the room or honouring the invitations they were given. The hierarchical position a leader holds immediately prompts people around them to put them on a pedestal even if the leader may not want it. So, being human- and value-driven makes their usually 'insignificant' action very 'significant'.

Modern employees want to see their leaders in action—leading by example and through the policies that run their organisations. When the leaders' actions in the policies that they frame actively work towards the things they say, they are viewed as worthy.

Many lessons can be learnt about leadership from Shivaji's life. His patience, his perseverance and his nimbleness are a few. Never the person to act rashly in saying the wrong thing or acting hastily, he had the knack to bide his time waiting for the right moment. This means a lot of patience was needed and for a person of action, surrounded by other strong-minded action and task-focussed persons, this could have been frustratingly long but this seems to have paid off in his lifetime.

Conclusion

While the Mughal depictions of Shivaji were largely negative, he was admired for his heroic exploits in battle and astute stratagem by foreign accounts. The person who brought the Maratha heartland together was a popular monarch, great organiser, military strategist, a skillful diplomat and a very shrewd administrator.

There are many lessons to be learnt from his life. Which one was the most useful for you?

Further Reading

Dr. Stewart Gordon, *The Marathas 1600–1818 (The New Cambridge History of India)* (Cambridge University Press, 2007)

R. C. Majumdar, *The History and Culture of the Indian People: Volume 7: The Mughul Empire* & *Volume 8: The Maratha Supremacy* (Bhartiya Vidya Bhavan, 2001)

Sir Jadunath Sarkar, *Shivaji and His Times*, (Orient Blackswan Private Limited, 5th revised edition, 2010)

Govind Sakharam Sardesai, *New History of the Marathas* (Gyan Publishing House, 2019)

Krishnaji Anant Sabhasad, *Sabhasad Bakhar* (1694): One of the earliest biographical narratives on Shivaji, written at Gingee fort in 1697 by a courtier of Shivaji.

AHILYABAI HOLKAR

> *Devi Ahilyabai Holkar, fondly referred to as Rajmata Ahilyabai Holkar (1725–95), is regarded as one of the finest female rulers in Indian history. As an astute and visionary ruler of the Holkar kingdom in the Malwa region, she spread the message of dharma and promoted crafts in the eighteenth century, leaving an indelible mark across India from Somnath in the west to Benares, to Badrinath in the north to Rameswaram in the south.*

Early life

Ahilyabai was born in 1725 in the village of Chaundi, in the present-day Ahmednagar district in Maharashtra. Her father, Mankoji Rao Shinde, was the patil (chief) of the village and homeschooled Ahilyabai to read and write despite women's education being taboo in that time.

Ahilyabai did not belong to a royal lineage and her entry into royalty was a twist of fate. Malhar Rao Holkar (1693–1766) was a subedar of the Maratha Empire. He was one of the early commanders to help spread the Maratha rule to northern states and was given the jagir of Indore to rule by the Peshwas, during the reign of the Maratha Emperor Shahu I. Malhar Rao Holkar spotted an eight-year-old Ahilyabai at a temple service feeding the hungry and poor while on his way to Pune. Immensely moved by the young girl's act of kindness and strength of character, he decided to ask for her hand in marriage for his son, Khanderao Holkar. Ahilyabai was married to Khanderao Holkar in 1733 at the tender age of eight. In 1745, she gave birth to their son, Malerao and in 1748, a daughter, Muktabai.

In 1754, Mughal Emperor Ahmad Shah Bahadur took the help of Malhar Rao Holkar to lay siege to the Kumher fort of Maharaja Suraj Mal who had sided with the Mughal emperor's rebellious general Safdar Jang. Khanderao Holkar, in the army of his father, was inspecting his troops on an open palanquin in the battle of Kumher when he was hit and killed by a cannonball. Ahilyabai was a widow at the age of twenty-nine.

Going against the prevalent tradition, Ahilya Bai was forbidden from committing Sati by her father-in-law, who became her strongest pillar of support at that time. Malhar Rao ruled for some more years, and upon his death, Ahilyabai's only son Malerao succeeded him at the age of twenty-one. However, Malerao was mentally unwell and died within a year of his succession.

Becoming a ruler

The fiefdom felt a strong vacuum, but Ahilyabai stood undeterred through all her personal losses, that too in quick succession. She channelled her grief into something productive by taking matters into her own hands for the sake of the administration of the fiefdom and the lives of her people. Already trained to be a ruler, Ahilyabai petitioned the Peshwa to take over the administration herself. Some objected to her assumption of rule, but the army of Tukoji Holkar (a military commander in her army) supported her leadership.

A letter to her from her father-in-law Malhar Rao in 1765 illustrates the trust he had in her ability:

> Proceed to Gwalior after crossing the Chambal. You may halt there for four or five days. You should keep your big artillery

and arrange for its ammunition as much as possible... On the march you should arrange for military posts being located for protection of the road.

The Peshwa granted her permission in December 1767, and, with Subedar Tukojirao Holkar as the head of military matters, she proceeded to rule the kingdom in a most enlightened manner.

The reign of Ahilyabai lasted for thirty years. This period has become almost legendary as a time in which perfect order and good government prevailed and the people prospered. She was a very able ruler and organiser, highly respected during her lifetime, and considered as a saint by a grateful people after her death.

Her accomplishments

Among Ahilyabai's accomplishments was the development of Indore from a small village to a prosperous and beautiful city. Her own capital, however, was in nearby Maheshwar, a town on the banks of the Narmada river. She built forts and roads in the Malwa region, sponsored festivals and gave donations to many Hindu temples. Outside Malwa, she built dozens of temples, ghats, wells, tanks and rest-houses across an area stretching from the Himalayas to pilgrimage centres in South India. Ahilyadevi also encouraged traders who brought her valuable revenue in the form of tolls and taxes. Her fair tax collection system helped farmers and cultivators to prosper.

Maheshwar became a melting pot for music and culture and she is known to have opened doors to stalwarts like the Marathi poets Moropant and Shahir Anantaphandi and the Sanskrit scholar, Khushali Ram. The capital was also known for its craftsmen, sculptors and artists who were paid handsomely for their work. The queen also encouraged the textile industry in the city. The famous Maheshwari sarees were probably created in her time.

The Holkar family did not use public money to meet their

personal and family expenses and used their personal funds instead. Ahilyabai inherited personal funds, which at that time was estimated to be Rs 16 crore. This would have been from income from lands that belonged to her. Ahilyabai used the personal fund in charitable works and her contributions went far beyond the Malwa region and extended to places like Kashi, Gaya, Somnath, Ayodhya, Mathura, Hardwar, Kanchi, Avanti, Dwarka, Badrinarayan, Rameshwaram, Puri and others.

Through public audiences held daily in her court, Ahilyabai addressed the grievances of her people and was always available to anyone who needed her guidance. Much of what we know of her is from a book on her by Sir John Malcom written about 40 years after her death. He says:

> Her first principle of government appears to have been moderate assessment, and an almost sacred respect for the native rights of village officers and proprietors of land. She heard every complaint in person; and although she continually referred cases to courts of equity and arbitration, and to her ministers for settlement, she was always accessible. So strong was her sense of duty on all points connected with the distribution of justice, that she is represented as not only patient but unwearied in the investigation of the most insignificant cases, when appeals were made to her decision.

She broke another tradition when she married her daughter to Yashwantrao, a commoner.

Ahilyadevi's borders were constantly attacked by the Rajputs and her best line of defence were the Bhils and Gonds. However, these tribal communities had not been treated with respect earlier and they, in turn, did not obey the kingdom's laws and were unpredictable. In an attempt to win their confidence, she granted them land rights and a right to a small duty on goods passing through their territories.

She was a shrewd ruler who realised early on the ambitions of the British. In a letter written to the Peshwa in 1772, she said, 'Other beasts, like tigers, can be killed by might or contrivance, but to kill a bear is very difficult. It will die only if you kill it straight in the face, or else, once caught in its powerful hold; the bear will kill its prey by tickling. Such is the way of the English. And given this, it is difficult to triumph over them.'

Ahilyabai was succeeded by her commander-in-chief, Tukoji Rao Holkar.

Life lessons

Finding stories of women rulers in history is rare, though most male rulers were supported by women. In the story of Ahilyadevi, we see a very principled ruler who did not flinch from standing up for what she believed was right. We can see some core beliefs she lived by, in her words and actions.

One was the belief in the concept of dharma—in thought, speech and action. She continued an ancient tradition of using temples as institutions to fund projects to fulfil the basic needs of the poor. Her courage to protect her borders, fight when needed and build alliances when required are also indicative of a shrewd survivor who did not flinch from taking tough decisions even when it was not personally convenient.

The business connection

Ahilyabai's life is comparable to that of a start-up that has to reach a point of sustainable scale. The creation of a start-up comes with a lot of excitement and promise and for a young, well-read girl, the excitement of making it in a man's world against all odds against much bigger rulers may have been similar.

The journey of a start-up is filled with achieving scale quickly and finding ways to fund them. Ahilyabai's use of temples to do her work of good governance and finding ways to fund her kingdom with alliances of traders and plugging loopholes in the tax collection system are comparable to the push in start-ups.

A difficulty with many start-up founders is their difficulty in letting go and holding on to some part of their ego. Ahilyabai, in her personal decisions, seems to have been philosophical and practical about this. Perhaps this was because of the many challenges she would have faced as a woman in a man's world.

Personal touch

Ahilyadevi's ability to put the larger cause above her own is an excellent mindset to adopt for those in organisations who only measure their development through the number of promotions they get. In my experiences as a coach, I have consistently seen coachees who have been successful are those who have constantly been flexible and curious about learning and contributing to various departments and geographies rather than staying only in one function. They have always put the need of the organisation above their own. I know of some who have even moved countries without the bat of an eyelid for the sake of the organisation. Such actions have added to their reputation as being reliable and trustworthy, which are critical for senior leadership. Ahilyadevi's success was because of others in the family, especially her father-in-law who constantly supported her. For preventing her from committing Sati, he too must have received condemnation from the more orthodox folks. If he had succumbed to pressure, Ahilyadevi would have never lived. As much as we celebrate successful leaders, it is vital to celebrate those who allow us to function effectively.

In my training sessions, I conduct an exercise wherein participants visualise and draw the critical incidents of their life as some sort of a painting. After sharing their life story with their colleagues, I then request them to share it with one person at home who is not connected to their workplace, but who is dear to them. A single father chose to do it with his driver. He explained to me that his driver would ferry his daughter from school and to all her classes and was very protective of the child, and him being there gave him great peace of mind about his daughter's safety. So, such people may not just be family but other service providers and they too deserve the appreciation for our professional success.

Conclusion

Centuries later, the brave and just queen's legacy lives on in the form of the numerous temples, dharmshalas and the large amount of social work that she dedicated her life to.

A commemorative stamp was issued in her honour in 1996 by the Indian government. As a tribute to the ruler, Indore's domestic airport has been named Devi Ahilyabai Holkar Airport. The Indore university too was renamed Devi Ahilya Vishwavidyalaya. To honour the memory of Ahilyadevi Holkar, leading citizens of Indore instituted an award in her name to be bestowed annually on an outstanding public figure. A statue of her can be found in the royal palace of Maheshwar.

Her ability to take a courageous stance and putting her duty above her rights are worthy legacies to emulate.

Further Reading

Eleanor Zelliott, 'Ahilyabai Holkar—A Magnificent Ruler, Saintly Administrator', *Manushi*, Issue 124 (May–June 2001), Retrieved on 17 November 2020 from http://www.indiatogether.org/manushi/issue124/holkar.htm

John Malcom, *A Memoir of Central India: Including Malwa, and Adjoining Provinces. With the History, and Copious Illustrations, of the Past and Present Condition of that Country* (Kingsbury, Parbury & Allen, 1823)

Narratives from the North

BABUR

> *Zahir Uddin-Mohamed, popularly known as Babur (1483–1530), was the founder of the Mughal dynasty in India. He was a descendant (through his father) of Timur (who founded the Timurid dynasty and was a great military tactician) and (through his mother) of Genghis Khan, the great Mongol warrior. Babur, which means tiger, was a brave and pragmatic ruler. He continues to be a hero to many and many verses from his memoirs, the* Baburnama, *are remembered even today.*

Early life

On 14 February 1483, in the hills of Turkestan, in the kingdom of Fergana by the Caspian Sea, a child was born to the ruler, Umar Sheik.

By the time Babur had turned eleven, his father had died, and he had been proclaimed the ruler, though he was still a minor. At this time, he was surrounded by many small fiefdoms, all under various members of his family who wanted to usurp his territory. Ruling Fergana, he set his sights on the kingdom of Samarkand, the most sought-after state in the region, which was ruled by his cousin. However, though he captured it after a seven-month siege in 1497, he lost Fergana that same year. Initially, he held on to Samarkand and as he tried to win back Fergana, he lost Samarkand too.

In 1501, he reconquered Samarkand but again it was short-lived and he left the region, leading the life of a wanderer around central Asia. During this time, as he coped with the loss of Fergana and Samarkand, he recognised the need for a disciplined and loyal army. These were some of the lowest moments of his life. Babur hated this time but also used it to keep himself filled with hope. Things changed for the better soon.

In 1504, he gathered an army, and marched on to Kabul, which had just undergone a change of ruler, and which his army was large enough to take and hold.

With Kabul as his base, he began taking the regions immediately around it. The position of Kabul with the mountains in the north meant they were safe from attacks for at least six months of the year due to the harsh winter. Kabul was also wealthy since it was a trading post in the caravan route from China to Europe. This was the time when he became a father. Between 1508 and 1519, he also acquired his first supply of guns and artillerymen and began to learn to use this novel and vital weapon. Babur clearly loved his time in Kabul and planted many beautiful gardens there. His autobiography reveals his deep love for plants, flowers, fruits and keen sense of interest in the observation of animals. Babur always identified himself with the cultured life of his Timurid inheritance and he was able to live this life in Kabul.

Babur tried hard to recapture Samarkand but did not succeed three times. The Shah of Persia was willing to help him but only if he became a Shia Muslim and this was unacceptable to Babur. Yet he did take his support and conquered Samarkand in 1511 but lost Persia's support when he refused to persecute Sunni Muslims in the region. Now expansion to the north or west was ruled out since it would mean antagonising the mighty Persian empire.

The only option was eastwards towards Punjab in the fabled land of Hindustan.

Babur realised that for a young man of ambition—he was only thirty-six—this was the best opportunity.

Babur's journey from the Caspian Sea to the Gangetic Plains

Babur prepared carefully for his subcontinental foray. He purchased guns and captured Kandahar so that as he progressed deeper into Punjab, he wouldn't lose Kabul. Kandahar was essential to hold on to Kabul.

In his first campaign in 1519, he came as far as the Jhelum river. The following year, he reached Peshawar but had to return to Kabul to supress an uprising. Then later, in 1520, he returned to the subcontinent and made his way till Sayyidpur (Eminabad in West Punjab). He was now determined that he would go as far as the Lodhi capital of Agra and occupy their old capital of Delhi. His opportunity came a few years later.

Events in the Lodhi kingdom also helped him. The Lodhi dynasty was slowly disintegrating. Factions were conspiring against Sultan Ibrahim who was not a popular ruler. He had jailed several senior courtiers and attempted to create a culture of fear but was not strong enough to keep his relatives and nobles in check. Confusion prevailed in the kingdom with many sensing an opportunity to claim the throne for themselves. One such person was Daulat Khan, the governor of Lahore. He invited Babur to invade and hoped that once victorious, Babur would make him the governor of Punjab.

In 1526, Babur came to Lahore, and marched to Delhi. Ibrahim Lodi's army of a 1,000 elephants and 1,00,000 men was not a full-strength one, but it was still much more than what Babur had. Even as Babur was on the march, there were attacks on Kabul by the Uzbeks. Other minor rebellions broke out in other parts of his Afghan possessions. His marching army was also constantly subject to attack by Gujjars in Punjab. Babur chose to ignore all of them for the time being, knowing that if he were to return to Kabul or turn his attention towards the raiders, the Delhi campaign would be a failure.

The two armies met at Panipat, and Babur, by dividing the army into various groups, used the old Mongol tactic of encircling the enemy army and closing in on them. He himself led the rear guard, using carts tied together as protection. By keeping the town of Panipat behind his section of the army, he ensured that Lodi had only one point of attack. The battle was over in half a day. At first, it was assumed that Ibrahim Lodi had fled. But towards the evening, his body was found by the side of his elephant, and his head presented to Babur. Babur ordered him to be buried in the battlefield and later had a tomb erected for him.

His son, Humayun, was sent on ahead to ensure that the wealth in Delhi remained secure. Humayun proceeded to block all roads leading out of Delhi.

Many of Babur's troops now wanted to go back. They thought this was one more raid to fill the coffers of Kabul. Babur, however much he liked Kabul, had bigger plans. To consolidate this new and prestigious acquisition, he had to deal with the Rajputs who had never been comfortable with the Lodhi kings and were waiting to assert their independence.

Battle with Rana Sanga and Dealings with Nasrat Shah

Rana Sanga was a Rajput chieftain who ruled the Chittor region of Rajasthan, and is mentioned by Babur as being among the noteworthy rulers of Hindustan at the time of his invasion. He was not considered an active threat at first. However, as Rana Sanga moved closer to Delhi, Babur realised something had to be done, and temporarily abandoned his fight against the Afghan Shahs of Oudh. He played the religion card to boost the morale of his troops. This was not a war to conquer but one against infidels, he declared. He dramatically threw away a cup of wine as a symbol of his adherence to his religion and as a mark of his determination to not drink till he won the battle. Rana Sanga was defeated at the battle of Kanwa, and was either killed or died soon after. Babur later entered into an alliance with Sanga's son.

Seeing the growth of Babur's military power, Nasrat Shah, the ruler of Bengal and the Afghan Shahs in Oudh and Bihar pledged their support to him. Very quickly, he became the undisputed ruler of the fertile Gangetic plain.

For the remaining four years of his life, he travelled across his new kingdom. He had to put down uprisings and even as he did so, he also found the time to write his autobiography that included fascinating descriptions of his new kingdom.

He died when he was only forty-five, his love for alcohol and his addiction to a drug he calls 'majun' having taken a toll on his health. It was a life interestingly lived, always exciting, never dull. He enjoyed his new kingdom for only four years but had carved a niche for himself by laying the foundation for an empire that was to prove far more long-lasting than that of his role-model ancestor Timur.

Life lessons

Babur's leadership traits can be gleaned from his thoughts as they have come down to us through his writings, which are frank, honest and contain a lot of information on not only what he thought but also on what he saw and heard in his short and exciting life.

Embracing innovative practices

Babur had a mind that was able to take quick, practical and creative decisions. He was a survivor and knew when to ruthlessly push his way through and when to build an alliance with the adversary.

The early years of his life, especially the ones he spent wandering in the mountains without a kingdom, must have shaped him. Looking at some of his decisions, we can glean some patterns.

Babur did not hesitate to try new ideas, even if they were expensive and difficult to obtain. His use of guns was instrumental in his victories in India. In today's world, it is the equivalent of scanning the radar for new technologies, new ways of doing things that others have adopted and quickly working with experts on applying it to one's own context. He also knew it wasn't about just buying equipment but also important to train his soldiers. Many entries in his autobiography mention the personal interest he took in understanding the new weapons and how they could work for him. He was a quick thinker. In the Panipat battle, using bullock carts tied up with one another to form a long wall of defence proved to be a decisive factor in his victory.

Dealing with others

Early experiences seem to have made Babur a pragmatic survivor who knew when to force compliance through fear and when to receive commitment through diplomacy. Such consistent behaviour from such a young person is rare.

At one end, we see him mercilessly beheading enemies and having their skulls piled up in a heap outside the village entrance as a warning. We also hear of how associates guilty of treachery were ruthlessly beheaded. But, on the other hand, we also hear of how, after he reached India, when Ibrahim Lodi's mother tried to poison him, she was not punished but relocated. Also, he was very careful in allowing defeated kings to rule, if they respected his authority. Even with the Rajputs, while he rallied his troops to fight for his religion, in his actual dealings, he was happy to allow others to practise their religion and was even curious to see their buildings and lifestyle. This ability to know when to punish and when to placate was instrumental in his success. Related to this was his courage to quickly take a decision and stick to it.

His relationship with his team (army)

The years of wandering made Babur acutely aware of the need to have a well-equipped army personally loyal to him. Personal loyalty may have been replaced by organisational or professional loyalty today, but Babur's close connection with his army is worth examining. He spent most of his life travelling from one campaign to another with them and had no hesitation in bonding with them, often through alcohol. While he was aware this was against the tenets of his religion, he had no hesitation in 'committing sin', as he termed it, because of the bond it built. Of course, this technique may not work for all but critical to his success was his ability to build a close connection with his team.

Persistence and pragmatism

Till he captured Kabul, Babur's life was filled with low points. Even after that, things were not always fine. Yet, in his life, we can see a man who was persistent and refused to give up—his desire to conquer Samarkand is an example. Yet, he was not adamant and knew when to quit. He understood that the Persians were very powerful, and looking at a fertile and law-abiding Punjab to the east was a practical decision for him to be remembered as a great king and not just one more petty ruler in central Asia. In the many raids he conducted, we discern a remarkable ability to judge when to push, fight and conquer, and when to glean that it was not worth the effort and close through a retreat or an alliance.

Documentation

Babur's *Baburnama* is probably the finest autobiography of that time. Through this we have minute information not only about the regions he travelled in but also about the life of the common people. History is usually the story of the rich and powerful but from his memoirs we get details even of the lives of the humble villagers. In it, he is brutally honest—he even writes truthfully about a young boy he was infatuated with, something that was unthinkable in those days. His work underscores the value of journaling. Several leaders I have worked with have been able to change their behaviour by carefully journaling what happened every day and reading it and reflecting on it periodically. What we watch we tend to change. Journaling becomes a way for us to become self-aware and, therefore, self-correct as well.

The business connection

Babur's lessons in creative thinking, building relationships and persistence and pragmatism are important qualities for all of us who seek to achieve professional success. His journaling was inspiring enough for many of his descendants to do the same and that has helped us understand the empire that they built and give us an insight into how they thought.

As the founder of a dynasty, these traits are particularly important for first-time entrepreneurs.

The early life of many entrepreneurs and leaders presents many instances of setbacks and failure. Walt Disney was told that he lacked imagination and had no original ideas. His first animation company went bankrupt and he succeeded in getting funding for Walt Disney Productions only after many unsuccessful attempts. Soichiro Honda's application to Toyota was turned down before he founded Honda. In all their cases too, you can see the same traits of Babur though their time and contexts were different. The same traits that made him famous also helped these leaders.

Building alliances with others and knowing when to cut one's losses and move on or persist are vital calls leaders have to take.

The situation, like in Babur's time, is complicated by never having 'enough' information. Taking a reasoned decision based on limited data is vital for leaders. Babur's ability to do this at such a young age is inspiring for leaders today.

Personal touch

I am reminded of a friend from childhood who was always very keen on health and fitness; he would always be playing a sport, working out in the gym and giving us long lectures on healthy eating when such concepts were not as well known back in the days when the internet had not yet changed our lives.

For a person like that to meet with an accident that left him in deep coma for many months and near paralysis would have been catastrophic. That too for an accident when he was on the right side but was hit by an under-aged driver under the influence of alcohol. With the support of family, friends and a committed medical staff, he slowly regained control of most of his muscles and despite his limp was able to transition from lifting weights to less intensive cardio and water-based activities. Moving out of a corporate job into the teaching profession meant a loss of income but a lifestyle that brought him closer to children gave him more positive energy.

His life and times are different from Babur but integral to his well-being and inner peace today are the same qualities of persistence, pragmatism and ability to lift himself out of extreme adversity with his inner conviction and the support of others.

Conclusion

Babur's was a life of adventure, which never ceased to lack excitement. He was skilled in military affairs and administration. He had, like all of us, desires and shortcomings, ups and downs. Babur is remembered for starting a dynasty but also for his own leadership qualities. Reading his story, in his own words, can inspire us on how to pick ourselves up from the disappointments of life with the help of others and find innovative ways to solve our problems.

Further Reading

Babur, and Annette Susannah Beveridge, *Bāburnāma: A Memoir* (Rupa, 2017)

Muzaffar Alam and S. Subrahmanyam, *The Mughal State: 1526-1750* (Oxford University Press, 2010)

S.M. Edwardes, *Babur: Diarist and Despot* (Universal Voice, 2010)

Mark Hay, 'The Conqueror Who Longed for Melons', *Atlas Obscura*, 2 February 2018, www.atlasobscura.com/articles/babur-mughlai-food-india.

JAHANARA

The immense literature available on the Mughals has paid more attention to the men of the royal family. While there are mentions of Mughal women, the information given is often very limited. This has resulted in not too many being aware of the women of outstanding ability who lived in Mughal times. One such woman was Jahanara Begum.

Jahanara (1614–81) was the daughter of the Mughal Emperor Shah Jahan and his wife, Mumtaz. She was the older sister of Dara Shikoh and Aurangzeb. Although she never became queen, her life and actions reveal her ability to navigate through a complex and rapidly changing environment stacked against women, to fulfil her own ambitions.

When she was born as a princess of the Mughal empire, it was already one of the most important in the world. Established in 1526, the empire controlled most of the Indian subcontinent with its population estimated to be between 110 and 150 million, over a territory of more than 3.2 million square kilometres. The Mughals set long-lasting precedents and created a number of institutions that balanced the needs and practices of local societies even as it established new administrative practices, leading to more systematic and centralised reign.

Status of women

In Jahanara's time, the position of women was largely subservient to that of men. However, women belonging to nobility did enjoy some privileges. The space allocated for women members of the royal household during the Mughal rule was called the harem, an Arabic term denoting a sacred and inviolable space. Women who were members of the imperial harem enjoyed a particularly high and exalted status within Mughal court life.

What shines through in Jahanara's instance is her ability to build and maintain relationships with different people, particularly critical stakeholders, at a time when the status of women was low.

In 1631, upon the death of her mother Mumtaz Mahal, Jahanara took over the responsibility of caring for her father. She inherited half of Mumtaz's movable property, which was worth Rs 1 crore then. The remaining property was distributed amongst the six younger children—Dara Shikoh, Shah Shuja, Roshanara Begum, Aurangzeb, Murad Bakhsh and Qudayyah.

The Mughal court of that time, like most royal courts in India, was filled with powerful, ambitious men who vied with each other for positions and honours from the monarch. The monarch was the sole authority and source of power and this meant intense competition not amongst just courtiers and the military but even among the king's own relatives, especially his sons. Also given that the Mughal system was one of allowing the fittest to succeed rather than an emperor planning his succession, sibling rivalry was intense. Palace intrigues and plotting fuelled this fire. In this toxic network of relationships with ambitious men, Jahanara, a woman, had to tread even more carefully. Her relationships with the key men in her family make for an interesting study, especially because those men were often bitter rivals of each other.

Jahanara and Shah Jahan

Jahanara was Shah Jahan's preferred child. And throughout his life she remained devoted to him. She is credited with bringing her father out of mourning and restoring normality to a court darkened by her mother's death and her father's grief. Shah Jahan often sought her counsel and elevated her status to first lady of the court. Jahanara was the favourite of many others too. Foreign travellers like Manucci and Bernier have expressed their liking for Jahanara in their accounts. Many foreign merchants and ambassadors also attempted to please Jahanara through gifts to gain the emperor's favours.

In 1644, Aurangzeb, Shah Jahan's youngest son, influenced by the unwise counsel of some of his advisers and through some of his own actions, incurred the displeasure of his father. His jagir and rank were confiscated. It was Jahanara who pacified Shah Jahan into giving back Aurangzeb his rank, office and position. In 1654, Raja Prithvichand of Garhwal sought the pardon of Shah Jahan through the offices of Jahanara.

In September 1657, when in Delhi, Shah Jahan fell ill. Dara Shikoh and Jahanara were by Shah Jahan's bedside all the time to make sure that opportunists did not take advantage of the situation. A month later, before leaving for Agra, Shah Jahan formally nominated Dara as his successor. In early 1658, Aurangzeb besieged his father at Agra Fort. In June 1658, Shah Jahan yielded and was imprisoned by Aurangzeb. Jahanara tried to persuade Aurangzeb again to release Shah Jahan, but to no avail. She then went into imprisonment with him and attended to her father till his last breath. Shah Jahan lived on for eight more years after recovering from the illness, but could not recover his power.

Jahanara and Dara Shikoh

One of the first joyous events that Jahanara arranged after her mother passed away was the marriage of her brother Dara Shikoh with Nadira Begum. Jahanara, like her brother Dara, was also spiritually inclined and both of them were initiated into the the Qadiriya order of the Sufis.

They shared similar tastes and views and were also patrons of the arts. Jahanara wrote *Munis-ul-arwah*, a biography of Sheikh Muinuddin Chishti, the philosopher and spiritual guide who had established the Chishti order of Sufism. Dara Shikoh's fascination for mysticism and eclectic Hinduism led him to write the theological treatise, the *Majma-ul-Bahrain* (Mingling of the Two Oceans), and translate the Upanishads into Persian.

Jahanara and Aurangzeb

In 1656, Abdul Qutb Shah, the ruler of Golconda who had not paid the due tribute, imprisoned the family of Aurangzeb's wazir, Mir Jumla. Aurangzeb, as the viceroy of Deccan, invaded Golconda and besieged it. Abdul Shah wrote letters to Jahanara and Dara. She intervened on his request and gained him a pardon from Shah Jahan.

Later in the decade, there was a war of succession between Dara Shikoh and Aurangzeb to obtain the throne of Delhi. In this war between brothers, Jahanara sided with Dara, while Roshnara Begum, the second daughter of Shah Jahan, championed the cause of Aurangzeb. As a partisan of Aurangzeb, Roshanara assisted him in securing the crown. She kept an eye on the affairs in the harem and gave Aurangzeb regular reports.

Jahanara tried to play the role of a peacemaker between the brothers but failed to make an impact. She admonished Aurangzeb for fighting against his eldest brother and advised him to observe the path of loyalty and obedience but to no avail. The battle of

Samugarh was fought between the brothers in May 1658 and Dara was defeated and later executed.

After ascending the throne, during the remainder of Shah Jahan's father's lifetime, Aurangzeb did not visit Agra. It was only after Shah Jahan's death in January 1666 that he decided to hold court in Agra. Aurangzeb's visit a month after Shah Jahan's death was mainly to win back the favour of Jahanara. He re-designated her as the first lady of the realm, with the title of Padshah Begum. Although she had sided with Dara Shikoh in the succession battle, it says much about her stature that after Shah Jahan's death, she was made the chief lady of the court by Aurangzeb and accorded every respect. Her power was such that, when Jahanara came back to Delhi, she lived in the late Ali Mardan Khan's enormous mansion, outside the confines of Aurangzeb's fort.

Jahanara's interest in trade and architecture was also deep. She owned a considerable number of ships and traded as an independent entity. She made colossal profits dealing with the Dutch and the East India Company. She designed the Chandni Chowk in 1600 and the garden known as Begum ka Bagh, which was later renamed as the Queen's Garden.

The business connection

Jahanara was not a queen and in spite of that, in a male-dominated world where the men she was connected to were bitter rivals, she was able to build alliances and achieve her own ambitions. This is the most fascinating aspect of her life.

The opportunities for growth for women continue to be a challenge even today. Studies show that women face discrimination from both men and women. In fact, in many organisations, women who reach the top tend to themselves discriminate against women owing to feelings of insecurity. The figures are striking when academically, women fare better than men but the flood becomes a trickle when it comes to leadership positions at the higher levels.

Gender equality in the workplace has been a focal point globally for the past few years. While there are prominent women private sector leaders in India, much remains to be done. Innovative polices are, of course, needed to bring women into the formal labour force but, more importantly, attitudes of both men and women need to change.

Could Jahanara herself have done more? Certainly. While she—through the force of her own personality—did carve a role for herself, it does not appear that much changed for the other women at that time in the court or elsewhere. Even so, while historians and feminists might judge her harshly for her lack of impact in the long term, one cannot deny that in her own life, even by today's standards, she is a role model of sorts—someone who balanced her needs with the needs of those around her. We might never fully know (owing to lack of information) why she did what she did and what her fears and challenges were and where she drew her energy from, but from the little information we have, there is enough to suggest that human nature—if it wants to—can triumph against as much of the odds as it is faced with.

Personal touch

To view Jahanara in a different perspective, I will not pick the example of a high-ranking CEO, but Malli, a humble flower seller in Chennai, who sold flowers door to door.

Abandoned by her husband and living the life of a single woman in a slum is, in material terms, the exact opposite of the luxuries that Jahanara enjoyed, but the determination to live her own life was just as evident. The luxuries or lack thereof did not matter, only the will to live on one's own terms. The flower seller did not achieve the power and money Jahanara did. No one will write books about her but for herself, given her background and what she had or did not have, she did well. That is really the inspiration—that each of us can, if we set our minds to it, see how we can overcome the glass ceilings and walls around us. Perhaps the glass ceiling was thicker for Jahanara or they were thicker for the flower seller but both chose to break them and yet not allow the shards to pierce others. They achieved greatness but not at the cost of others. This can be one lesson from Jahanara's life. That you can, even with restrictions around you, fulfil your destiny and do so without harming others.

Stories like those of Jahanara or the flower seller remind us that even in an unequal world, not only can women work towards what they want but they can also find courage and resolve to deal with the (greater number of) hurdles and yet carve out their niche—whatever it might be.

Conclusion

Jahanara's tomb is a simple yet elegant marble enclosure with a tombstone that carries her own verse:

> He is the Living, the Sustaining
> There cannot be any other curtain of my tomb except the
> humble covering of grass.
> Grass alone is sufficient to cover the grave of a poor person,
> as I am
> Disciple of the Khwaja Moin-ud-Din Chishti,
> Daughter of Shah Jahan the Conqueror
> May Allah illuminate his proof.

Her epitaph expresses her wish for her grave to be covered with grass, like any other ordinary grave. Ironically, this wish came from the 'First Lady of the Empire'. In choosing not to occupy the centre stage, but yet make a mark, Jahanara inspires us even today.

Further Reading

S. Blake, 'The Patrimonial-Bureaucratic Empire of the Mughals', *Journal of Asian Studies*, 39(1), 1979, 77–94. p.82

Abraham Eraly, *Emperors of the Peacock Throne: The Saga of the Great Mughals* (Penguin Books India, 2000)

Ruby Lal, *Domesticity and Power in the Early Mughal World* (Cambridge University Press, 2005)

Soma Mukherjee, *Mughal Women: Royal Mughal Ladies and Their Contribution* (Cyan Publishing House, 2001)

Ira Mukhoty, *Daughters of the Sun: Empresses, Queens and Begums of the Mughal Empire* (Aleph Book Company, 2018)

Jadunath Sarkar, *History of Aurangzeb, vols. 1-3* (M.C. Sarkar & Sons, 1917)

AURANGZEB

> *Mohiuddin Muhammad Aurangzeb, Mughal emperor Shah Jahan's sixth child, was born in 1618. After defeating his brother Dara Shikoh, in the war of succession, in 1658, Aurangzeb wrested the crown from his father. Historian Audrey Truschke says, 'Aurangzeb was arguably the most powerful and wealthiest ruler of his day. His nearly fifty-year reign (1658–1707) had a profound influence on the political landscape of early modern India, and his legacy—real and imagined—continues to loom large in India and Pakistan today.' During his lifetime, the extent of the Mughal empire was more than 3.2 million square kilometres—territorially, it was at its largest.*
>
> *The period of the Great Mughals, which began in 1526 with Babur's accession to the throne, ended with the death of Aurangzeb in 1707. Within about fifty years of Aurangzeb's death, the massive Mughal empire that had grown manifold because of his untiring efforts had disintegrated considerably.*
>
> *Why the empire that he worked so hard to build to such an extent disintegrated so quickly after his passing makes for useful lessons for those of us who want to create an impact or leave a legacy.*

Early life

One of the earliest demonstrations of Aurangzeb's courage and fearlessness took place when he was fourteen. On the banks of the Yamuna in Agra, all of Shah Jahan's court was arrayed in a pavilion, watching an elephant fight, when one of the elephants ran out of control. The prince is said to have met it head on and came out unharmed.

When he was eighteen, the young prince was appointed the viceroy of the Deccan region where he served from 1636 to 1644. During the years that he spent in Deccan and the other provinces of the empire, Aurangzeb distinguished himself as an able administrator. R.C. Majumdar writes, 'Undaunted bravery, grim tenacity of purpose, and ceaseless activity were some of his prominent qualities. His military campaigns gave sufficient proof of his unusual courage, and the manner in which he baffled the intrigues of his enemies shows him to have been a past master of diplomacy and statecraft.'

Just like the greatness of a brand today is judged by the number of countries it is present in and the number of users it has, for a long time, the geographical size of a kingdom has been an important criterion to determine its greatness and importance. Aurangzeb was able to build his empire by waging war with other kingdoms in India.

Reign

Conflict with Marwar

After the death of Raja Jaswant Singh in 1678, the ruler of Marwar (also called Jodhpur) and a former ally of Dara Shikoh, Aurangzeb wanted to occupy the kingdom. He was not in favour of the ruling family since they had earlier supported Dara. In 1658, Aurangzeb conquered the kingdom of Marwar. It is said that the then Marwar king was advised to conduct a night raid but believed it was not appropriate in the Rajput code of war and was defeated by the Mughal army. After annexation, Aurangzeb destroyed several temples to stamp his authority. But he had to continue to fight bitterly to retain the territory till his death in 1707, as rebellions against his rule kept erupting. His son and successor Bahadur Shah I recognised Marwar as an independent kingdom in 1709.

Conflict with Mewar (Udaipur)

At the time of Aurangzeb's accession, there were three important Rajput kings—Rana Raj Singh of Mewar/Udaipur, Raja Jaswant Singh of Marwar/Jodhpur and Raja Jai Singh of Jaipur. Their relationship with Aurangzeb was harmonious at that time, though in the past some had supported his brother. Years before, Akbar had harmonised relationships with the three kingdoms and Shah Jahan, while not befriending them as much as Akbar had, maintained a cordial relationship.

But Aurangzeb's move towards a fiercely theocratic state after his enthronement ruffled feathers.

When Aurangzeb occupied Marwar, Mewar came out in support of Marwar. This was a flashpoint. Secondly, Aurangzeb's new policy of reimposing jizya also caused the three kingdoms to turn against him.

Aurangzeb re-imposed jizya in April 1679, more than a century after Emperor Akbar had abolished it in 1564. The issue of jizya is a complex and contentious one with many claims and counterclaims. Some say that while non-Muslims had to pay jizya, Muslims had to pay zakat, a tax that a Muslim had to pay as charity, thereby levelling the field. Others counter that jizya was a way for Aurangzeb to force people to convert to Islam. Aurangzeb was no doubt motivated to re-introduce it to fund his enormous military expenses but coupled with his moves towards a theocratic state that overturned the more tolerant image Akbar had created for the Mughals, it upset many people. The tax also hit the poor where it hurt—probably even more than the temples he demolished.

Yet another flashpoint was when Aurangzeb's son Prince Akbar who had originally been left in charge of Mewar and later replaced by Prince Azam, joined hands with the Rajputs. Their joint forces clashed with the Mughal forces. It was the beginning of a conflict that continued till Aurangzeb's death, with the kingdoms never fully submitting to Mughal rule.

Conflict with Bundelkhand

Champat Rai, the Rajput ruler of Bundelkhand, got into a conflict with Aurangzeb and committed suicide in order to save himself from imprisonment. Later, his son Chhatrasal defied the Mughals and set up an independent state in eastern Malwa. He was a hero in the eyes of the people of Bundelkhand and Malwa. He was hailed as the 'champion of the Hindu faith and Rajput honour'.

The Rajput policy of Aurangzeb produced disastrous consequences for the Mughal Empire. The money and energy of the army and the monarch was spent fighting to conquer or retain this region and it was a constant pressure point for Aurangzeb. While it can be said that this is the case for all expansionist kings, but when one compares his policy with that of Babur or Akbar, it appears that Aurangzeb may have benefitted if he had worked out a less military-focussed and a more diplomatic relationship with the Rajputs. That may have not made them such bitter foes to his rule.

Besides the Rajputs, Aurangzeb also alienated a number of other kingdoms and communities in India.

Sikhs: The conflict between the Sikhs and the Mughal rulers began during the reign of Jahangir when Guru Arjun Dev, the fifth Guru of the Sikhs was executed. The conflict became even more intense during the reign of Aurangzeb.

The ninth Sikh Guru, Guru Teg Bahadur (1664–75) was met

by a deputation of Kashmiri Brahmins who complained of the atrocities of the Mughal governor in Kashmir. The Guru promised to protect them. Later, he was summoned to Delhi by Aurangzeb on a pretext, but when he arrived, he was asked to abandon his faith and convert to Islam. Upon his refusal, he and his associates were arrested. He was later executed on 24 November 1675 in public at Chandni Chowk, Delhi.

Jats: There were multiple revolts of the Jats of Mathura against Mughal tyranny, the first one in 1669 being the most bloody. It ended in 1688 when the Jat leader was caught and beheaded. The immediate cause was the local governor Abdun Nabi Khan's overenthusiastic desire to literally follow his emperor's command to 'root out idolatory'. In removing a railing given to the temple by Dara Shikoh and building a mosque at the site of a ruined temple, he galvanised the existing discontent of the common people against many other issues of the religious policy that had been simmering for a while. The zamindar of Tilpat saw this is an opportune moment and raised an army and fought back. He lost his life and the revolt was ruthlessly crushed. The defeat of the Jat community only spurred further revolts and they continued to rise and had to be put down for a long time after that even though the area was conquered by the Mughals. The Mughals held on to the region with great difficulty and had no choice but to allow one part of it to become an independent kingdom.

The Marathas: Aurangzeb's relationship with Shivaji is discussed in the chapter on him (Chhatrapati Shivaji Bhonsle). But, post Shivaji's death in 1680, Aurangzeb killed the Maratha king Sambhaji (Shivaji's son), and the conflict with the Marathas continued. After Sambhaji's death, the struggle was carried out by his widow, Tara Bai. In spite of his best efforts, Aurangzeb failed to crush the Maratha resistance. The annexation of Bijapur and

Golconda also destroyed the check on Marathas. A lot of money was wasted in the Deccan wars.

The largest extant of the Mughal empire

By 1690, Aurangzeb's empire comprised the territory from Kabul to Chittagong and from Kashmir to the Kaveri. The Mughal Empire had become too large to be ruled by one man or from one centre. His enemies rose on all sides; he could defeat but not crush them forever. Lawlessness reigned in many parts of northern and central India.

Even though under Aurangzeb's rule, the empire reached its greatest extent, he facilitated the decline of the empire by leaving an overstretched empire with too many disgruntled subjects to his successors. His expansion was unbridled and poorly planned, over-extending the Mughal state and weakening its financial stability. Aurangzeb failed to realise that the vast Mughal empire depended on the willing support of the people.

In every dynasty, the first few rulers have focused on the task of building. But later, complacency and rigidity and the mindless following of templates and rules has set in, paving the way for the system to atrophy and decay and eventually be overcome by a smaller, nimbler and younger power. Both Aurangzeb and Shah Jahan were the architects of the collapse of Mughal Empire.

In the quest to expand his territories and build the empire, one of the biggest mistakes that Aurangzeb made was to constantly work alone. Leaving a legacy seems to be a powerful motivator for many. Some adopt short-term techniques, others more long-term ones. But a legacy can be created only with others, and when they have been able to feed the hunger of others and work with them, rather than alone.

Where did he fail?

Consolidating conquered land: Aurangzeb worked tirelessly, displaying exemplary personal leadership to wage war and defeat those who rebelled against his rule. However, he did not learn to consolidate what he had won at great financial and personal cost.

There are two ways in which he could have consolidated. One was to plan his succession and ensure that his successor consolidated what he had grown. This would have been difficult to expect from him since the Mughal tradition followed the old Mongol way of allowing the sons of a dead ruler to fight among themselves and allow the eventual victor of this tussle to rule. So, succession planning was out of bounds for him. His life had taught him not to trust his kith or kin and he centralised most of the power in his hands. He alienated many of his children and wives, driving some into exile and imprisoning others. Aurangzeb's focus on reducing the threat of rebels and expanding his empire distracted him from the increasing threats to him from the western part of this kingdom, and left the empire in a desperate state after his death in 1707.

The other way to consolidate would have been to build a more efficient administration during his own lifetime. This he could have done only with the support of his subjects. His inability to do so provides us with a glimpse into his personality.

Aurangzeb in his adulthood comes across as a deeply pious, almost fanatically frugal person who seemed to eschew the wealth and pomp that came with his position. His condemnation of the ways of the wealthy would have alienated him from the elite of the lands he conquered. His insistence on his faith against other faiths to the extent that he even alienated his subjects who subscribed to other branches of Islam caused him to be reviled. It is possible that it was not so much what he did—for he wasn't the only king to pillage and plunder—but how he made his subjects feel that contributed to his inability to consolidate during his time and has tainted his legacy in the long-term.

He did not trust his children to rule and he did not have enough trusted advisors to consolidate administration. The Mughal centre lacked an institution with which it could advance an alternate paradigm for rule. Therefore, it was compelled to relax its hold over former dominions and concede ground to more vibrant regional formations. It resulted in the emergence of a slew of 'successor states', namely, Awadh, Bengal, Hyderabad, the Marathas and the Sikhs.

His relationship with his Hindu subjects: Aurangzeb was born a Muslim, like every other Mughal leader, and practised his inherited religion throughout his life. We do have evidence of temples he has destroyed but we also have evidence of the land grants he made to temples. So, it is not possible to brand him as a bigot. In one of his early acts as emperor, Aurangzeb issued an imperial order (firmaan) to local Mughal officials at Benares when he learned that Hindu residents who were in charge of the temples had been harassed. The imperial order directed his officials to halt any interference in the affairs of local temples. He issued similar imperial orders to protect several other temples. An imperial order sent out in 1680 specified that a Hindu ascetic—Bhagwant Gosain—who lived on the banks of the Ganges in Benares not be harassed.

Aurangzeb also gave grants for maintaining temples and donated land to Hindu communities. In 1691, he conferred eight villages on Mahant Balak Das Nirvani of Chitrakoot in order to support the Vishnu Temple there. A stone inscription at this temple still shows that it was commissioned by the emperor himself. In 1698, Aurangzeb gifted rent-free land to a Brahmin named Rang Bhatt in eastern Khandesh in central India.

Hindu bureaucrats were at the core of the Mughal empire during Aurangzeb's rule. He employed more Hindus in his imperial administration than any prior Mughal ruler. Aurangzeb had Hindu generals like Raja Jai Singh and Jaswant Singh as his military generals. Both of them played a key role in his campaigns against the Ahoms and Sikhs. Hindus were also present in the state treasury. In his administration, the state policy was formulated by Hindus. However, this can be argued as more political expediency since many of the educated, experienced men aware of local dynamics needed for a bureaucracy would have been Hindu anyway.

Life lessons

The biggest lesson from Aurangzeb's life is how chequered or contested a legacy can be! He is either reviled or seen as a sad figure. He ruled over a huge territory. He led by example and was very frugal in his personal life. It can be argued that many things he did were actions other ambitious kings would have taken. However, the way he did it, even today, after generations, angers and divides. It would be interesting to conduct an analysis of whether Aurangzeb would have been financially better off if he had fully focused on his military strategy and not pursued his religious policy. The religious policy served as a source of discontent that constantly incited people to revolt, and subduing those revolts cost the treasury a lot of money that could have been spent elsewhere.

Aurangzeb was the most powerful of all the Mughal emperors of India when he ascended the throne in 1658 and is today one of the most reviled of all the Muslim rulers in India. Aurangzeb's historical legacy is widely contested in public discourse. The Mughal emperor is often seen as a tyrannical Muslim fanatic, who ordered the destruction of Hindu places of worship, though scholars like Audrey Truschke insist that this depiction of Aurangzeb is misleading.

Aurangzeb was extremely ambitious but not a visionary. No other Mughal emperor, with the possible exception of Akbar, spent as much time on the battlefield and won as many battles as Aurangzeb. He expanded the boundaries of Mughal rule and made it the most extensive empire in Indian history but failed to leave a legacy. Consolidation of what you have is critical for leaving a lasting legacy.

The business connection

Consolidating an organisation is vital for business. Consolidating means getting people to embrace the new identity, the new teams and locations as part of the whole. It could be at an emotional level of getting people to embrace the new shared identity of a larger team. It could also be at a process level where there are common new or altered process for the way things have to be done. Essentially, it is about culture. Aurangzeb acquired territory but did not achieve integration. Hence, the dismemberment of the Mughal empire after his death.

Mergers and acquisitions are doomed to fail if merging organisations are not integrated. The unsuccessful AOL–Time Warner merger is an example where the Time Warner president later admitted that he had underestimated the importance of culture. This can also happen to start-ups that have scaled up too quickly. They have to learn to run before they learn how to walk and their legs are just not fit enough yet.

At an individual level, it can apply to young managers who have been promoted too quickly or who have to suddenly take on a much larger responsibility because of a colleague who has left or a big client that has just been won.

In all these cases, consolidation is vital. What are the tactical things that Aurangzeb could have done that today's leaders overseeing mergers and acquisitions should do? They need to communicate to their teams and make them aware of the change, much more than they think necessary. Fears need to be allayed even if there may not be enough knowledge of what the new normal is going to be. From this, a clear sense of what we should think, do and say differently can be created. This can even be as basic as a PowerPoint slide that lists out issues with a clear response guideline of 'what we said or did before' and 'what we will henceforth say or do' in the adjacent column. Meeting each of the people from the new team, reassuring them and listening and summarising and doing whatever else *they* need is vital. The more that is done to improve trust and present clarity, the faster the consolidation will happen.

The HP-Compaq merger was, at one time, considered to be a disaster but since then, it has become a fairly successful one. Experts say that one of the reasons the ill-effects were reduced was that HP really listened to ideas from Compaq and the necessary changes were made. HP also benefitted from the enterprise technology of Compaq. Closer home, you will find every leader who has won a new client or has been appointed to lead a new geography would have taken specific steps to consolidate before moving on. Which is what HR folks also mean when they say, 'You just got your promotion now, why are you looking for one more so soon?' What they really mean is to ask if you have consolidated your position before you move on.

Personal touch

In my HR experience, I have had the chance to attend many retirement functions and while in public, speeches are delivered, gifts given and food and drink enjoyed, in many cases, as the retiring individual stepped into the car to go home—and often it was my duty to take them home that evening—private conversation would turn into deeper reflection.

I remember one conversation with a long-timer from the auto industry. The man had tears in his eyes for he had seen the company grow in size but had never seen his children grow in the same way. All his time and energy had been spent only on his work life. The thought of retirement was scary for him for he had no life apart from work and with constant travel, he had largely been an absent father and husband who had only financially provided for his family.

With good intentions, I asked him what he thought his legacy would be and how his team would remember him and he burst into tears. He regretted that throughout his life at work, while he had helped his team, his focus had always been only on technology and while his legacy was about technical improvements to the product, he was afraid that nobody on his team would miss him and his home would be the same too. 'I have never spent much time with my children in their growing years, now they are all married and live abroad, I don't even know how to build a connection now and I can't undo this,' he said with tears welling up.

Conclusion

As you read about Aurangzeb, you get a sense of many facets of his personality. There is the austere leader who practises what he preaches, shuns wasteful trappings and is very humble. You also see the determined, tough person who brooks no interference in getting what he wants the way he wants. You also see a courageous and brave warrior.

One would like to think that on his deathbed, Aurangzeb himself saw that the empire he had built with so much hardship was going to vanish quickly. While this is just speculation, we do know the fate of his hard-fought empire after him. The map that shows how the Mughal Empire shrunk is a lesson for us to consolidate every small gain we achieve before we seek out the next.

Further Reading

Athar Ali Athar, *The Mughal Nobility under Aurangzeb* (Asia Publishing House, 1970)

M. Bhargava, ed. *The Decline of the Mughal Empire* (Oxford University Press, 2014)

K.B. Brown, 'Did Aurangzeb Ban Music? Questions for Historiography of his Reign', *Modern Asian Studies*, 41/1 (2007): 77–120

Abraham Eraly, *Emperors of the Peacock Throne: The Saga of the Great Mughals* (Penguin, 2000)

R.C. Majumdar, et al. *An Advanced History of India* (MacMillan, 1958)

Jadunath Sarkar, *History of the Emperor Aurangzeb* (r.1658–1707 A.D.) Translated edn. of Saqi Mustaid Khan's *Ma'asir-I Alamgiri*, (Royal Society of Bengal, 1947)

Audrey Truschke, *Aurangzeb: The Man and the Myth* (Penguin Random House, 2017)

Audrey Truschke, *Aurangzeb: The Life and Legacy of India's Most Controversial King* (Stanford University Press, 2017)

M. Maqbool, 'A caricature of "Aurangzeb The Bigot" serves many modern political interests in India: An interview with the historian Audrey Truschke', May 2017, *The Caravan*

A. Mukul, 'Aurangzeb, A Stranger No More' (Review of Audrey Truschke's book), 4 March 2017, *The Hindu*

A. Raman, 'Aurangzeb is a severely misunderstood figure: Interview with Audrey Truschke', 4 September 2015, *The Hindu*

A. Roychowdhury, 'In new book, a side of Aurangzeb India is not familiar with', 15 June 2017, *The Indian Express*

U. Sen, 'Aurangzeb's villainisation is bad history but a good storyline', 12 August 2018, *The Telegraph*

THE FIRST FIVE SIKH GURUS

Sikhism, one of the youngest religions of the world, originated in Punjab towards the end of the fifteenth century. The word 'Sikh' means a seeker of the truth. The Gurus, in their life span of 239 years, developed a very practical religious order. Sikhism is open to all through the teachings of its ten Gurus enshrined in the Holy Book, Sri Guru Granth Sahib, drenched in practical wisdom and moral and spiritual principles, providing positive direction to the life of seekers. The main virtue of Sikhism is its simplicity, preaching a message of devotion and remembrance of God at all times while opposing superstitions and blind rituals. It strongly advocates the idea of universal peace, integrity, brotherhood, liberty and contentment.

In the early years, the religion had Gurus who wielded political, social and cultural authority over their followers. All of them displayed leadership qualities and their shared legacy gives us lessons for how to create and maintain an emotional connect.

Guru Nanak Dev (1469–1539)

Guru Nanak Dev, the founder of the Sikh religion, was born in Talwandi (near Lahore) in a Hindu Khatri family. From a very young age, his inquisitive mind and a desire to explore led him away from the conventional path. He refused to wear the sacred thread and instead remarked that he would wear the true name of God in his heart as protection. Popular folklore recounts that as a young child, he described an analogy between the first letter of the alphabet and the mathematical version of one, as denoting the unity or oneness of God.

He was employed by Daulat Khan, the governor of Sultanpur, as a storekeeper. It was during this period that Guru Nanak disappeared during one of his daily ablutions and re-emerged after three days a changed man. He would then go on to remark: 'There is no Hindu and no Musalman', that stressed the unity of humankind.

Guru Nanak Dev laid down three basic principles that continues to serve as a novel and uncorrupted approach towards life, spirituality and God.

- *Naam Japo*: Believing in and meditating the name of one true God to control human vices
- *Kirat Karo*: Earning and living through honest means
- *Vand Chakko*: Sharing a part of such earnings with others and compassion towards all.

At a time when rulers exploited the common people, Guru Nanak Dev travelled widely on a mission to disseminate the spirit of universal brotherhood, spreading the message of peace, compassion, righteousness and faith. He made four distinct journeys, in the four different directions (Udasis), preaching the message of God at the grassroots level, envisioning a classless and casteless society.

Guru Nanak Dev organised Sikh societies into assembly places called Dharamsalas where Sikh congregations and religious gatherings were held. He introduced the practice of community kitchen where people from all castes and creeds sat together to eat without any distinction of social hierarchy. The first known centre established by Guru Nanak Dev was at the abode of Sajjan (a thief), which was previously used for looting innocent travellers.

Nanak evoked his spiritual conscience through his discourse and transformed him into a real 'Sajjan' (good man).

When Nanak had worked as a storekeeper, he had dedicated a large part of his earnings to feed the poor and the hungry. In his spiritual discourses, he emphasised the concept of sharing one's income earned through honest means and discouraged the notion of earning through unfair means and then offering a part of it as charity or penance. During one of his travels, he preferred to stay with Bhai Lalo, who was a low-caste artisan, as he earned his living in a just way with his own labour and efforts, declining the invitation of a high-caste rich landlord, Malik Bhago, as the latter lived by exploiting the poor and abusing the power he possessed.

Guru Nanak Dev never ignored or ostracised people who were enveloped by vices and sins but worked to reform them into good human beings. He transformed the lives of folk people like Sajjan, the cheat, Malik Bhago, the exploiter of the poor, and the downtrodden, Nur Shah, the practitioner of black magic, Kauda, the head-hunter, Duni Chand, the hoarder of wealth, to quote a few. Guru Nanak Dev accentuated the value of virtues of the human character and advised control of vices through self-examination and self-realisation.

In his later stages of life, Guru Nanak Dev regularly tested his disciples as well as his sons on their devotion, dedication and perseverance towards the mission. Once, he asked his disciples and his sons to carry three bundles of grass, which were wet and muddy, for his cows and buffaloes. Lehna was the only one to obey the master and carried the grass bundles on his head without bothering that his clothes were getting soiled. Guru Nanak Dev was impressed with Lehna and bestowed upon him the Guruship. Lehna later assumed the name Guru Angad Dev. To this day, Sikhs consider the three bundles as important symbols of spiritual affairs, temporal affairs and the Guruship. The successive Gurus were always selected on merit and judged on their spiritual vigour and aptitude to fulfill the responsibilities of the mission.

Guru Angad Dev (1504–52, Guru from 1539–52)

Before becoming a Sikh and being renamed as Angad (from 'Ang' or part of God) by Guru Nanak, Guru Angad Dev was known as Bhai Lehna, a religious teacher who followed the Shakti tradition in Hinduism. He became a disciple of Guru Nanak in his late twenties and built on the foundation set by Guru Nanak.

Guru Angad Dev popularised the script of Gurmukhi (foundation of Punjabi script) for the masses. He created a separate and distinct identity of the people by giving them a means to read their own language, thus making them knowledgeable for unhampered growth and development. This helped to raise the morale of the downtrodden and secured the unhindered development and expansion of Sikhism.

No country, organisation or mission can succeed without a strong education system. Guru Angad Dev gave immense importance to the education of children and opened many schools for their instruction. For the youth, he started the tradition of Mall Akhara (wrestling arenas), motivating people to lead fit and healthy lives as means to achieve higher goals.

At a time when women were not allowed to move out of their houses, Guru Angad Dev gave equal status and freedom to his wife Mata Khivi. She worked along with Guru Angad Dev and enhanced the role of women in the court of the Guru. The institution of free community kitchen, langar, was maintained and supervised by them to promote the acceptance of social equality.

He established new centres of Sikhism, strengthening its base and developing its unique religious identity. He also collected the facts about Guru Nanak Dev's life from Bhai Bala and wrote the first biography of Guru Nanak Dev, thereby being instrumental in spreading his ideals.

Guru Amar Das (1479–1574, Guru from 1552–74)

Before he converted to Sikhism, Amar Das was a religious Hindu Vaishnavite and had undertaken pilgrimages to the Himalayas. On his return, he heard Bibi Amro, the daughter of Guru Angad, singing a hymn of Guru Nanak. He adopted Guru Angad Dev as his spiritual guide at the ripe age of sixty-two. His focus was on serving his Guru with a humble disposition, unflinching zeal and pure dedication. Once when Datu, son of Guru Angad Dev, who was frustrated for not getting the Guruship, kicked Guru Amar Das with his foot when he was seated on the 'Gurgaddi' (the Guru's seat), the Guru did not utter even a single word of anguish. Rather, he sympathised with him, saying that his foot must have been hurt by his hard bones.

Guru Amar Das possessed strong organisational skills and he systemised the organisation of the community kitchen in a very meticulous manner. He made it mandatory for each of the followers and visitors to first have food from the free kitchen and then join the congregation, Sangat. Even Emperor Akbar had to abide by this rule. Emperor Akbar sat for langar with the common man and then was allowed to join the congregation and meet the Guru. Akbar was impressed with this system that encouraged tolerance and acceptance across all lines. Guru Amar Das then persuaded Akbar to waive off tax on pilgrimages for non-Muslims.

Guru Amar Das established the Manji system to propagate Sikhism in a systematic and planned manner. He divided Sikh congregation areas into twenty-two Manjis and a local preacher (Masand) was made in-charge of each Manji. He personally trained the group of followers, which included women, to attend to the spiritual needs of the people. The Masands travelled far and wide to spread the gospel of Sikhism. It was a great step in decentralisation.

He wrote and compiled hymns into a 'Pothi' (book) that

ultimately helped create the *Adi Granth* and also established rituals for weddings, festivals (Diwali, Maghi and Baisakhi) and funerals.

Guru Amar Das constructed a baoli (deep well) at Goindwal Sahib, which provided safe drinking water to people and helped to create an eco-friendly environment. The baoli at Goindwal became a pilgrimage centre for the first time in the history of Sikhism. It also helped in boosting the identity of the new sect. He was also responsible for selecting the site for Harimandir Sahib.

Guru Ram Das (1534–81, Guru from 1574–81)

Guru Ram Das was born as Bhai Jetha in a Hindu family in Lahore but was orphaned at a very young age. He and his grandmother moved to serve Guru Amar Das when he was twelve. He accepted Guru Amar Das as his mentor and married one of his daughters. As with the first two Gurus of Sikhism, Guru Amar Das chose Bhai Jetha over his two sons as his successor and renamed him as Ram Das in 1574.

Guru Ram Das laid the foundation of Amritsar on 13 June 1577 and called upon the Sikh devotees across regions to make donations by organising Masands as revenue collectors for meeting the requirements of the community kitchen and construction of a holy tank. He invited traders to settle around the city and it suited them due to its proximity to Lahore. The Masand institutional organisation famously helped grow Sikhism in the following decades, but became infamous in the era of the later Gurus, for its corruption and its role in financing rival Sikh movements in times of succession disputes.

Guru Arjan Dev (1563–1606, Guru from 1581–1606)

Guru Arjan was born in Goindwal to Bibi Bhani and Guru Ram Das. He was appointed as the Sikh Guru in 1581 after the death of his father, becoming the first guru to be born into a Sikh family. He was preferred over his eldest brother Prithi Chand, while the middle brother Mahadev lived the life of an ascetic. Based on certain accounts of official Sikh history, Prithi Chand was embittered and started one of the major subsects of early Sikhism. This subsect came to be labelled as the Minas, literally 'unscrupulous scoundrels', by followers of Guru Arjan and accused of conspiring with Muslim leaders against his own brother and later Sikh Gurus as well.

Guru Arjan Dev gave a distinct identity to the Sikhs by completing the Harimandir Sahib at Amritsar and by compiling the *Adi Granth*, which was later called *Sri Guru Granth Sahib*. He was a dynamic personality—social reformer, spiritual mentor of high order, moral disciplinarian, diligent organiser and a great litterateur.

Guru Arjan Dev observed tolerance and respect for all religions and castes. He invited Mian Mir, a Muslim saint, to lay the foundation of the Harmandir Sahib at Amritsar. The building was designed in such a way that it had doors in all directions, signifying its acceptance of all the castes and every religion. On the completion of the Harmandir Sahib he honoured the dedicated and low-profile disciple Bhai Banno for his efforts by placing the first platter of the feast before him.

Guru Arjan Dev systematically compiled the hymns of the preceding four Gurus in their original form in the form of a scripture known as *Adi Granth*, thereby preserving the treasure of great wisdom for the future generations and dissemination of the spiritual knowledge. At the same time, it threw light on contemporary political and social life. He compiled the hymns of the earlier Gurus, he added his own compositions as well as the celestial utterances of Sheikh Farid, Bhagat Kabir, Bhagat Ravi Das, Dhanna Namdev, Ramannand, Jai Dev, Trilochan, Beni, Pipa, Surdas and some others. All these saints belong to different times, beliefs, sects, and both 'high' and 'low' castes.

The First Five Sikh Gurus

Guru Arjan Dev highlighted the importance of good company, as one would be able to keep the mind marching towards the path that is true and righteous, being freed from the influence of evil desires and malefic thoughts through right mentorship, example and guidance.

He took special care of lepers who were treated as outcastes by the society and not cared for even by their own relatives. Guru Arjan Dev reorganised the system of Masands to perform an additional role as revenue collectors and directed his followers to contribute one-tenth (Dasvand) of their earnings for social and religious causes. The concept was to share earnings of the more fortunate people with the less fortunate and spread prosperity amongst all.

After Guru Arjan completed and installed the *Adi Granth* in the Harimandir Sahib, Akbar was informed of the development with an allegation that it contained teachings hostile to Islam. He ordered a copy be brought to him. Guru Arjan sent him a copy with a message that he would find three things upon going through it—truth, peace and contemplation in the support of all humanity.

Guru Arjan met the Mughal emperor in 1598. This meeting likely influenced the later development of the Sikh martial tradition. Guru Arjan Dev called upon his followers to learn horse riding to train for potential onslaughts of the Mughal emperors, as he could visualise the impending times. He encouraged them to take up horse-trading as a profession. He wanted his followers to be ready for all types of contingencies and situations.

Upon Jahangir's ascension to the throne in 1605, the Mughals, now alarmed at the expansion of the Sikh religious order, would embark on persecution of the Sikhs. Jahangir ordered the imprisonment of Guru Arjan Dev in 1606 in Lahore fort. He was ordered to remove certain passages from the *Adi Granth*, which

Jahangir felt were objectionable to Muslims. On the Guru's refusal to do so, he tortured and executed the Guru. In his martyrdom, he conveyed the message to his followers that they must always face bravely evil, cruelty, oppression and injustice. This is considered a watershed event in the political history of Sikhism.

Leadership lessons

Several lessons can be learnt from the Gurus as a whole and from individual Gurus. At a broader level, the institution's success is definitely because of the ability of the Gurus to set strong personal examples of service to the larger community that is a hallmark of the Sikh community even today. Langar or the meals served in gurudwaras for those in need is a well-known example. This unbroken spirit of being of use to the larger community came from small but deeply symbolic actions each Guru did in his lifetime. They became ways to lead by example. Leaders need to constantly show such examples of 'walk the talk' and all the Gurus did this in many different ways.

From a personal perspective, the Gurus enjoyed deep connection and followership because of their leadership by example and putting the cause of their community over their own. This created a sense of trust in their relationship with their followers. Studies have shown that when leaders set a personal example, they not only receive voluntary reciprocal behaviour from their team but they also tend to integrate the team better.

The third lesson to learn is the ability of Gurus to manage an organisation of people. Their excellent communication and their constant travel to meet and build rapport are important aspects to pay attention to. Their patience, persistence, ability to analyse and decide quickly are admirable and all of this was done without the superior communication and data analytics facilities we have today. Managing scale was more complex then than it is today and the Gurus were able to do it primarily because of the relationships of trust they had built and that came through their practice of leadership by example and also by living the values they stood for.

When it comes to building and leaving a legacy, it is the small things that make a big impact. I once worked with a chemical manufacturing company that was run by the second generation. The company had grown by leaps and bounds in a short period of time largely because of the single-minded focus of the founder. We had a strategy planning session I facilitated and when the session got over, as we were leaving, I saw him patiently putting all the sketch pens into their covers and rolling up the unused chart papers and asking the other employees to take it back. It may seem like a trivial action but he explained to me, 'Throughout the session we were emphasizing on finding ways to reduce costs and work on environmentally friendly options. If I don't do this, how can I expect them to?' Sure enough, as others saw this, they too helped and the company did exceed its targets. Even when his son was young, he got him to work across all departments in all shifts to train him up to eventually take over and when the time was right, while he continued to be the chairman, the son took over management. At this juncture, I have found retired leaders not having other passions beyond work, but fortunately, this leader developed an interest in collecting art and focusing on CSR activities. He said, 'If I don't keep myself busy, I will become a nuisance to the younger members of the company; let them learn from their own successes and failures, it is time for me to reinvent myself.'

Further Reading

Kartar Singh Bhalla, *Sikhism* (Star Publications Pvt. Ltd., 2002)

Harish Dhillon, *The Lives and Teachings of the Sikh Gurus* (UBS Publishers Distributors Pvt. Ltd., 2005)

K.S. Duggal, *Sikh Gurus* (UBS Publishers' Distributors Pvt. Ltd., 2010)

Kusum Ghatage, *Ten Gurus of the Sikhs* (Bharatiya Vidya Bhavan, 2005)

Max Arthur Macauliffe, *The Sikhs: Their Religion, Gurus, Sacred Writing and Authors* (Cosmo Publications, 1989)

Khushwant Singh, *A History of the Sikhs Vol 1: 1469–1839* (Oxford University Press, 2004)

Khushwant Singh, *The Sikhs* (HarperCollins, 2006)

https://www.sikhiwiki.org/

*Stories
from the
South*

MARTHANDA VARMA

Marthanda Varma (1706–58), the ruler of the kingdom of Travancore, is today known as the 'Maker of Modern Travancore'. The Travancore region was originally under the Chera kings who ruled from about the third century BCE for many centuries and were one of the longest ruling dynasties of India. It is believed that Kerala owes its name to the term 'Chera'. The region was then dotted with many small kingdoms and was seldom attacked from outside due to the Western Ghats, thick forests and the many rivers that made it difficult for large armies to advance in the region.

Kerala, however, had a connection with the outside world through the Arabs, Portuguese and Dutch because of the coast and the spice trade. They partnered with local kings and on occasion were rulers in Kerala as well. By the fifteenth century, the two most important kingdoms of the Kerala region were Calicut and Travancore.

Among Marthanda Varma's greatest achievements was to steer Travancore through its relationships with the Dutch, Portuguese and the East India Company and the various complex connections with the big and small kingdoms of Kerala. His ability to keep his kingdom independent and strong through all of this was his biggest achievement.

At the beginning of his rule, Travancore was besieged by various others who had some form of control over the affairs of the state. There were incursions by the Madurai Nayaks, almost annually.

> *The English, with a factory at Anjengo, were not military allies, but had still not developed political ambitions, which would come with the Carnatic wars in the middle of the eighteenth century. The Dutch were allies of Attingal, the more powerful state, with whose Rani they had entered into treaties.*
>
> *Varma quelled the growing Dutch influence on the Western coast, strengthened ties with the English, absorbed various smaller surrounding kingdoms into Travancore, established a kingdom that eclipsed those that lay around it and turned Travancore into what would be termed a 'model state', 200 years later, by the British.*

Initial years

The time preceding Marthanda Varma's accession was a time of Dutch power and constant clashes between the various Kerala kingdoms.

Marthanda Varma was heir apparent to his uncle, Rama Varma, and had some amount of political influence during his rule itself. In 1723, he signed a treaty with the British and influenced his uncle to negotiate a treaty in 1726 with the Madurai Nayaks to stop their incursions.

In 1729, Marthanda Varma succeeded to the throne. At that time, administrative affairs were in a bad state. The Dutch were moving to capture all of Kerala, and had under their control various forts and towns, and their control was apparent over a few local rulers. In the late seventeenth century, the Yogakkar, the royal caretakers of the Padmanabha Swamy temple in Thiruvananthapuram, had divided up the administration of temple lands into eight districts, entrusting a Nair family with each district. These families were together known as Ettuvittil Pillamar (ettuvittil is derived from 'ettu veedu' which in Malayalam means eight houses). By the time Varma ascended the throne, they had become very powerful and were a potential source of opposition to him.

With these various problems before him, Marthanda Varma began building up a kingdom that would be the basis for one of the most powerful of the princely states during the time of the British.

Consolidation of power

Marthanda Varma's first task was to consolidate his power. He had to contend with the noblemen of the Ettuvutil Pillamar, as well as the Ettara Yogakkar (the temple management board who had assigned the lands to the Pillamar). At the time of his accession, his cousins, Padmanabhan Tampi and Raman Tampi, had stirred up trouble by claiming power, through the patriarchal descent system (even though Travancore was matriarchal). The Yogakkar and Pillamar supported them. Their support was important since they wielded much social and political power and could make or break kings.

Marthanda Varma dealt with this through a variety of actions. The Madurai Nayak general, who had been called by his cousins, the Tampis, was bribed, and sent back. The Tampis were then captured and executed on the orders of Marthanda Varma. The Pillamar were also put to death. Their property was then confiscated, declared state property and their families sold into slavery. He thus ruthlessly destroyed the system that threatened him.

To improve the army, Marthanda Varma reorganised it with modern methods of warfare and by thinking up new battle strategies. He capitalised on the then tradition of all noblemen having military training schools in their villages and used that system to train local men more rigorously to minimise state spending on the training of soldiers. Before launching his many campaigns, he reduced expenditure and oversaw the creation of a more efficient tax collection system.

Expansion

With his army in good shape and well-funded, from 1730 onwards, Marthanda Varma began a policy of expansion, taking over neighbouring kingdoms, using his modernised army, as well as through other means. Though they resisted, over the next few years, Attingal, Kottarakara, Colachel, Desinganad (Quilon or Kollam), Kayamkulam, Elayadathu Swarupam, Ambalapurza, Tekkumkur, Vadakkumkur and Minachil fell.

Even though he faced setbacks, like at the battle of Kayamkulam where he was unable to win, Marthanda Varma did not let that bother him, and always moved ahead, proving that being assertive was beneficial. The kingdom of Attingal was integrated with his own kingdom through a treaty. As both rulers hailed from the same extended family, the treaty declared that only the sons of Attingal Ranis would be Rajas of Travancore. The rest were predominantly military conquests.

Protection from incursions

The Madurai Nayaks had always bothered Travancore, making incursions into the region almost every year. Marthanda Varma had convinced his uncle to sign a treaty with Madurai that would give them an annual tribute to stop the incursions. Later, during his own rule, he had to deal with the Nawabs of Arcot, and the polygars/local chieftains of Tirunelveli, who constantly moved against his eastern territories. He dealt with them firmly and always sent them back, either by buying them off or by sending troops and chasing them out. This went on sporadically all through his reign.

In 1729, just before he ascended the throne of Travancore, a civil war broke out in Madurai. This worked well for Marthanda Varma, who welcomed refugees into his territory. The income so gained went towards maintaining a mercenary army.

Defeat of the Dutch

The Dutch had been in Kerala since the sixteenth century. They began their expeditions in 1603, and, by the early eighteenth century, began expanding trade relations and consolidating their position. Over the next 100 years, their political control also increased considerably, especially in present-day Kochi and Kollam and they replaced the Portuguese as the European colonial power on the Malabar coast. However, with the advent of Marthanda Varma in 1729, their hopes of ruling the Malabar region were shattered. He signed non-political treaties with them, like the one that guaranteed them the right to build a pepper storehouse at Pandaratourte and at Karunagapalli, but not rule over the people there. Frustrated, they began allying themselves with those that Travancore was hoping to conquer, including Quilon/Desinganad and Kayamkulam.

After the Battle of Colachel against Elayadathu Swarupam in 1741, where the alliance of the Dutch and the local army was beaten, Marthanda Varma refused to recognise the right to succession of the senior princess, after the death of the king in the jails of Travancore. Meanwhile, the Dutch continued to shelter her in Cochin. This led to Marthanda Varma seizing Dutch forts within his territory. As a result, the Dutch landed naval troops from Ceylon at Colachel. They then began moving up the coast, conquering territory as they moved ahead. Though Marthanda Varma sent a Nair regiment of 1,000 men and entered into an alliance with the French at Mahe, he was not able to do much, as he was in the north, annexing further territory. Instead of giving up hope, and the south, he put the northern conquests on hold, and moved south to deal with the new threat, arriving just in time to prevent the Dutch taking his capital, Padmanabhapuram.

After a two-month long battle, the Travancore army finally won, as a result of their strategy and assertiveness. They placed reeds disguised as guns in the line of attack, and the Dutch wasted their ammunition shooting at them. A well-timed cannon ball set the Dutch ammunition on fire, and the Travancore soldiers immediately surrounded the Dutch, forcing them to surrender. And thus Travancore earned the distinction of being the first Indian kingdom to have won a war against a European one.

In 1748, Marthanda Varma signed a treaty with the Dutch, wherein they promised not to disturb English trade or their factories at Anjengo, Vizhinjam and Edava, and ensured their neutrality in any of Travancore's future wars.

One of the unforeseen gains to Marthanda Varma after the Battle of Colachel was to secure the services of D'Lannoy, a Dutchman who was captured after the war and taken hostage. However, he soon proved useful to Marthanda Varma as a leader of his army, and even helped train and improve it. He was made 'Valia Kappithan' (Senior Captain), and was one of Marthanda Varma's reasons for success, leading the army even after Marthanda Varma's death in 1759.

Padmanabhaswamy proclamation

In 1750, Marthanda Varma did something that left an extraordinary mark on his kingdom. He dedicated the state to Padmanabha Swamy, the chief deity of the Travancore royal family. The Padmanabha Swamy temple, in Thiruvananthapuram (where the Travancore capital was shifted), became the place where all future rulers of Travancore were anointed. (This temple became famous a few years ago when massive treasure, spanning various centuries, from Marthanda Varma's time all the way back to Roman coins, were discovered in a locked underground vault.)

This meant that Varma ruled, as would his successors, on behalf of the Lord. The main implication this had was that it pacified all those who were hurt at having been so brutally and suddenly annexed into the kingdom. People were more likely to respect Marthanda Varma's decision now that he was acting 'on behalf of God'. It meant that a rebellion, or any attack on Travancore, was an attack against Lord Padmanabha himself. With one simple declaration on 3 January 1750, Marthanda Varma had ensured that political instability would reduce drastically.

Though the Travancore rulers had considered themselves servants to Lord Padmanabhaswamy since the fourteenth century, this made it formal and binding.

In fact, before the proclamation, the various annexed states of Travancore repeatedly rose in rebellion. After the announcement, there was only one major war against Travancore, in 1754, when Cochin and the Dutch allied for one last confrontation against Travancore at Ambalapuzha, which ended with the Cochin Raja suing for peace.

End of reign and death

After 1754, Marthanda Varma's reign was mostly peaceful. He signed a treaty against the Zamorin with Cochin in 1757, and this ensured peace in Travancore, a peace that would be maintained till the end of the century.

On his deathbed in 1758, Marthanda Varma is supposed to have instructed his successor, Rama Varma, to maintain cordial relations with the British, and keep them on his side as allies. This would prove to be good advice since the British left Travancore alone even as they went about annexing other states in southern India.

Life lessons

Marthanda Varma's singular defining characteristic is pragmatism and assertiveness. Right from the beginning of his rule in 1729, he asserted himself as a leader to be looked up to and someone to be relied on, as an able general, as a strategist and as a conqueror. His reign set the foundations for the state of Travancore in the twentieth century, a state that often outshone its larger neighbour, Mysore, and most of the 565 other princely states. He went about his tasks at a measured pace, first consolidating, then bringing his army to an efficient level, waging wars where needed, bribing or entering into treaties as required and finally dedicating his kingdom to a larger-than-life presence to make consolidation and succession for the long term easier. His dedication of the state to the temple was a masterstroke, especially at a time when religion was a deeply emotional subject. The equivalent today would be the vision statements of companies.

By today's standards, his methods of bribing and execution will definitely not work. However, his ability to be focused on what he wanted and get it even if it meant he had to give up his ego and need for self-glory is worth examining.

The business connection

Marthanda Varma was able to consolidate, aggressively reach scale through consolidation and finally create a compelling emotional connect for the future security of his kingdom once his ambition had been achieved.

This connects with any leader who would have, on assuming office, built networks for support, looked at how to improve the bottom line and then aggressively push for the top line. Usually, leaders start with a compelling vision that they communicate. Varma seems to have used the vision more for the future than for growth.

Varma was not the first king to connect with religion. In several kingdoms, rulers have used temples and religion to legitimise their power and propagate their welfare measures. Marthanda Varma, by officially formalising the connection as a means for reducing the threat of further attacks and for ensuring that future dismemberment of the kingdom would be prevented, made an astute move. There is no doubt that he would have been deeply driven by faith but we cannot forget the possible political motives as well.

Problems and opposition are inevitable whatever the plan. How we deal with it is critical. In some cases, we can fight for our idea and convince others; in other cases, we can build alliances inside and outside and modify the idea but still implement it. This is what he was very good at.

Personal touch

I have found, especially at the middle management level, smart performers who have a strong task focus become impatient for the next promotion even before a year has elapsed from their previous one. They would do well to learn from Marthanda Varma. In their new role, they could look at how to bring in better operational efficiencies, build a new or deeper connect with their peers inside and outside their company and with their team members. Instead of thinking in this direction, they aspire to quickly move to the next rung of the ladder. But creating a solid foundation before moving higher would be a surer way to success.

Most companies have a vision statement but very few really go beyond displaying them as posters or stationery. An organisation I worked for made the vision more real by organising a regular 'values' day, where the key values of the company would be remembered by colleagues sharing stories of how they practised them and where they struggled to do so. This made the values not just the company's but also their own. Values can be a great way to build deeper commitment and reduce the ego affecting our actions, similar to Varma's action of declaring the lord the ruler of his realms. They could also become a legitimate way to influence others for a higher purpose.

Conclusion

Marthanda Varma's actions give us much food for thought and action. Aurangzeb, for instance, would have learnt a good lesson from him or perhaps Marthanda Varma knew his story. Who can tell? What we do know is how Marthanda Varma lived and there are enough lessons to be learnt.

Further Reading

Manu S. Pillai, *The Ivory Throne: Chronicles of the House of Travancore* (HarperCollins, 2015)

A. Sreedhara Menon, *A Survey of Kerala History* (DC Books, 2017)

Mahadev Desai, *The Epic of Travancore*, 1937, www.archive.org/details/Travancore/page/n81

TIPU SULTAN

Tipu Sultan (1750–99), also known by the epithet 'Tiger of Mysore', was an eighteenth-century ruler based in what is today Karnataka. He ruled the kingdom of Mysore from his capital in Srirangapatna, an island in the river Kaveri. At its height, the kingdom included much of present-day Karnataka and parts of Kerala, Telangana, Andhra Pradesh and Tamil Nadu.

The origins of the Mysore kingdom go back to the time when it was a feudatory of the Vijayanagar empire based in Hampi, Karnataka, between the fourteenth and seventeenth centuries. The Wodeyar kings were the hereditary rulers of Mysore who, with the decline of the Vijayanagar empire, set themselves up as independent monarchs. In the 1740s, the then Mysore ruler noticed the skill and talents of a young, illiterate boy called Hyder Ali who hailed from an Arab tribe called the Quraish. The boy quickly rose through the ranks in the Mysore army and became its 'Dalavay' or chief commander.

Impressed with his administrative and military skills, by 1761, Hyder Ali was made the 'Sarvadhikari' or chief minister. Hyder Ali was known to have remarkable memory power, military courage and a talent for numbers that helped him to rise to power in the Mysore court, eventually overthrow the Wodeyars and establish himself as the ruler of the Mysore Kingdom.

He was succeeded in 1782 by his son Tipu Sultan. Like his father's reign, Tipu's reign too was marked by frequent battles with

> *neighbouring kingdoms. Among the entities that Tipu frequently clashed with was the East India Company, whose star was on the ascendant and who aspired to extend their power and influence in the Indian sub-continent.*
>
> *Tipu earned his name, the 'Tiger of Mysore', because of his skill on the battlefield, where he managed a large army, and fought to defend his kingdom. Tipu defeated the British in the Second Anglo-Mysore war (1782–84), conducted regular raids into Company territory and clashed with neighbouring kingdoms in his bid to widen his territorial control. Eventually, in the Fourth Anglo-Mysore War (1798–99), Tipu was defeated by the British.*
>
> *Tipu's most powerful adversaries were the British and although he was ultimately defeated by them, he is remembered as one of the early Indian kings who fought against them.*

The life and times of Tipu

Tipu ruled from 1782 to 1799. It was not uncommon those days for neighbouring kingdoms to be frequently at war with each other—either to add more territory and increase revenue or to protect themselves from enemies across borders. As a young ruler who had inherited his kingdom from his self-made and intelligent father, Tipu too was ambitious to expand his territory. To this end, he undertook several military expeditions.

Kerala campaigns

Years before Tipu's Kerala campaign, Hyder Ali had also made an incursion into the region. At that time, in the mid-eighteenth century, the many kingdoms that controlled different parts of the territory that is now known as Kerala were vying with each other for control. The Zamorin of Kozhikode (Calicut) was the most ambitious and a number of smaller kingdoms were either in an alliance with him or fearful of an invasion by him. A succession dispute in Kannur (Cannannore) had other kingdoms taking sides with the parties involved. The Portuguese and Dutch traders were also constantly playing one ruler against the other to wrest greater trading concessions for themselves. The region was clearly in disarray.

Kerala held two attractions for Hyder Ali. It gave him access to Mahe, the French colony from where he could get military equipment to fight the East India Company and the Marathas and access to revenue from the spice trade. However, entry into Kerala was difficult. The Western Ghats were a barrier. But since the region around Coimbatore and the Palakkad Gap was under the control of Mysore, in 1766, Hyder Ali made the decision to invade.

Accompanied by a young Tipu who was entering a battleground for the first time and with an invitation from the Kannur king in his kitty, Hyder Ali entered the region. His army was better trained and he consolidated his gains quickly and prevented his adversaries from reaching out for help. Eventually, the Zamorin was defeated and he blew up his palace and immolated himself.

Some years later, Hyder's preoccupations with the Marathas, and later his death, gave Kozhikode the opportunity to declare independence.

In 1783, Tipu marched into Kerala to re-establish control. Most of the other local rulers either submitted to his superior army or fled. Some sought the help of the East India Company to regain their kingdoms. By 1789, most of Kerala was under Tipu.

Between 1783 and 1789, Tipu effected many administrative measures in the Kerala region that helped improve economic prosperity. He introduced an extensive system of roads that helped in the transport of produce faster and more efficiently. He made the sale of pepper, cardamom and sandalwood (the three most lucrative products) the monopoly of the State. The new roads helped move these quickly and safely to his warehouses in Vadakkara, Kozhikode and other places. The produce was purchased directly from the farmers at a fair price, which reduced the role of middlemen or foreign traders who, guided by their desire to make a high profit, forced farmers to sell at low prices. His land tax reform meant direct collection of tax from the farmers who felt more dignified by this compared to the past when tax was collected by the upper-caste landlord.

However, his ruthless treatment of those who opposed him, especially the upper class of rulers and landlords, turned many people against him. While this was the usual practice in those days amongst kings, Tipu's not being from Kerala made the difference starker. His unwillingness to honour the traditional role of temples to be asylums for those fleeing from political persecution and forced conversions led him to be feared and hated. These emotional issues for most people outweighed the benefits that accrued from his efforts to improve the economy.

When he marched towards Travancore, an ally of the East India Company in 1788/9, the Company took it as if it were an attack on themselves and prepared for war. Luckily for them, they had agents in the court of the Peshwa, leader of the Maratha confederacy, and the Nizam of Hyderabad, and these agents plotted and secured a deal with those leaders. These enemies of Tipu had fought each other before, as well as the East India Company. Their hatred of Tipu, and their need to claim lands taken by him and his father decades ago, brought them closer to the their enemy, the Company. Things did not quite work out for Tipu owing to these factors.

Tipu's wars with the Marathas and the Nizam of Hyderabad

Between 1785 and 1787, Tipu fought a war with the Marathas who had allied with the Nizam. This war proved to be disastrous because, though he won most of the battles and repulsed his enemies, it effectively meant that he had distanced two of the most powerful kingdoms in South India.

The Nizam's wealth was enormous, as was his army, and the Peshwa was the leader of the Maratha confederacy that spanned a vast expanse of modern India, from the Krishna to the Ganga. Tipu tried to curtail his campaign against these two empires once he understood that he couldn't hold out forever against their might. At one point when he held the upper hand, he called for surrender and opened negotiations. However, it was too little, too late, and the effects of his distancing these leaders proved disastrous in the long term.

Tipu in peacetime

Art and architecture bloomed in Tipu's rule. As for engineering and architecture, his palaces and forts are proof enough of his interest in these matters. Tipu's summer palace had a system that allowed him to draw in the waters of the Kaveri into the bathing room, with a provision for heating it there. His revised coinage (that were beautiful and well-designed) and calendar are proof of his innovative abilities. Tipu also encouraged crafts and agriculture. Industry was promoted as well, with innovative weapons casting being an area of focus. His penchant for administration and protocol meant that nothing went undocumented, allowing later historians to accurately study the many aspects of his rule.

Relations with the French

As a child, Tipu had been educated by French military officers in the pay of his father. The French were bitter enemies of the British in India and it was natural for him to turn to them for support.

The French were the ones he constantly appealed to for military aid, as he saw them as the primary enemies of the English. But Tipu could not quite understand that the French, on their part, did not seem to have the same level of trust in him. In 1787, he sent a delegation to King Louis XVI and while they were received well, they came back without having been able to conclude any sort of firm alliance. It would be another decade before he got any French help and that too was half-hearted.

The Third Anglo-Mysore War broke out in 1790, and the French, when sent a letter from the British, as to their status, assured them that they were neutral. Clearly, Tipu's attempts to build an alliance had made no headway. In fact, he was so desperate for support that he was even cheated by a pirate who claimed to be a representative of France.

Tipu and the East India Company

The East India Company did not view Tipu as its biggest adversary at the onset. Mysore, in their view, was just another kingdom to be conquered. But Tipu and Hyder were much feared, as they conducted regular raids into Company territory in the Madras Presidency and this was an economic drain to the Company whose sole aim was trade and, therefore, profits. The loss of capital and productivity because of Tipu hampered them considerably. Soon, with the onset of the Third Anglo-Mysore War, they rushed to the help of their ally, Travancore. With an able leader, Lord Cornwallis, they put together an alliance with the Nizam and the Marathas that was more than Tipu could handle.

The East India Company went into this alliance by promising its allies the return of territory captured by Hyder and Tipu. They also offered them the assistance of two British battalions in their attack. But, most importantly, they gave them a chance at revenge.

The three armies attacked Tipu's empire from various sides, and with no aid coming from the French, Tipu was defeated and a humiliating treaty imposed on him. Later, in 1799, in what was the Fourth Anglo-Mysore War, Tipu was killed and the Wodeyars regained the throne of Mysore.

Tipu's undoing

Tipu was a fierce warrior with a powerful army. However, he lived at a time when the East India Company was growing in power, and looking for opportunities to expand their territory and influence. They worked hard on their foreign policy, always trying to keep many kingdoms in an alliance with them. This worked well for them whenever an enemy state (or sometimes, even an ally) threatened them.

During the early part of Tipu's reign itself, he had alienated the Marathas, Travancore and the Nizam of Hyderabad. Under usual circumstances, this would have been the normal course of history, but for Tipu this was not helpful since this did not help him in his bid to overcome the British, who were, by far, his most powerful adversaries. Given their superior military power, he could not defeat them on his own.

Tipu's military strategy seemed to be more short-term. He often focused on quick gains of land or wealth, rather than a secure empire. By looking at how he could boost his financial position immediately, he did not explore how he could leave a lasting legacy. His constant raids and battles meant people in nearby regions lived in constant fear. Also, his military expeditions meant long absences from the capital. His policy towards religion was one of political expedience rather than either religious harmony or the pitting of one against the other. All in all, he seems to have been more of a feudal autocrat. Personal loyalty and regional power were important to him and he did whatever, in his opinion, was important for that in the short term.

So, in the end, Tipu was left, without allies, to fend for himself. He had made things complicated by preferring loyalty over criticism and was surrounded by loyal generals who dared not speak against him.

Life lessons

Tipu was young, ambitious, courageous and well-educated. He had the benefit of a well-trained army and loyal and intelligent supporters. Initially, he achieved military success and instituted many administrative reforms. But a key takeaway from his life is that continuous success without allies and friends is impossible.

Someone is always on the lookout to exploit your shortcomings and it is not prudent to assume that no one will. However, the way to overcome that is to build firm networks of supporters, especially those who are geographically proximate—not just people sitting in your next cubicle or cabin or your immediate peers from within your team and those teams that are most relevant for your success. The trick is to cast the net far and wide.

Tipu comes across as an extremely determined man. For a ruler of his means and position, to take on the British army and to give them a tough fight is praiseworthy. But if that had been backed with his allying with his own neighbours or working with them more diplomatically and letting words rather than cannons do the talking, he may have been more successful and certainly less-hated in the long term.

What Tipu did not do in building allies, his adversaries, the British, did. They put together a group of people who had no experience of working together previously and had, in fact, worked against each other to take down a common enemy or, in other words, achieve a common purpose. Impossible things and targets that seem difficult can be done with proper planning and determination. Without planning, they never would have got together the necessary rulers' assent or waged a proper war against Tipu. The behaviour of the Kerala kings, the Peshwa and Nizam tell us that people will unite easier if there is a common goal.

Hate them or love them, one has to view the East India Company's efforts at surviving in a complex, alien land like eighteenth-century India in the right perspective.

The business connection

It is said that there are no permanent friends or enemies, only permanent interests. Tipu Sultan might not have heeded the wisdom implicit in this adage and nor indeed did the Peshwas and the Nizam, as it turned out to their detriment, much later. But business history is replete with instances where companies demonstrate that they are not unnecessarily hampered by the past. Yesterday's collaborators could well be today's competitors and may well end up becoming collaborators yet again tomorrow in their quest for greater profits.

A case in point is the automobile industry. The industry started as one where the car maker made all the parts themselves but today, the components are so complex that it is impossible to produce a car or even a part of it without many alliances with several companies. Several HR leaders have often remarked therefore, that to learn about the intricacies of professional relationships, the auto industry is the best place to start!

An example of the indispensability of such relationships is that of the US automaker Ford Motors and its Indian partner, Mahindra & Mahindra. They came together in the early Nineties to assemble Ford's 'Escort' sedans at Mahindra's manufacturing facility at Nashik, Maharashtra. They then went on to set up a manufacturing facility in Chennai, Tamil Nadu, a few years later, only for Mahindra to exit completely from their joint venture in 2005. But in October 2018, the two companies announced that they were coming together to work on BS-VI compliant engines*

---

*Engines that emit less nitrogen oxide and, therefore, more environment friendly.

for the Indian market and telematics solutions for cars that would enable passengers to surf the net. This should hardly surprise anyone, as every strategic action that these two companies have taken over the last twenty-five years or so in their on-off business association has had a compelling business logic.

In the early Nineties, Ford was looking for a quick entry into the Indian market and Mahindra provided them with a framework with their manufacturing facility. For Mahindra too, it made sense. If they had nursed any ambitions at all of entering the passenger car business, what better way to wet their feet in the business than with a global auto major such as Ford? By 2005, both parties had travelled some distance in the passenger car market in India. Ford was not yet offering the full range of models that they were capable of bringing to the Indian market. But the few that they had introduced had given them some traction with the Indian consumer. Mahindra too had launched a few models of their own, thanks to their experience in building cars in the company of Ford.

Each was ready to launch themselves in the Indian market on their own by that time. Equally when they came together in 2018, it was dictated by business compulsions in an industry that had become a lot more complex than the one when both companies went their separate ways some years previously. The latest news in late 2021 indicates a change yet again with Ford deciding to move their automobile production out of India.

There is a great deal of pressure on organisations for quarter-on-quarter improvements and the financial investments needed for companies to gain the cutting edge are significant. In this situation, it is often difficult to think long-term, especially when costs are high and the future is uncertain. This is why, more than ever before, thinking beyond the short term and building alliances are vital for long-term profitability, even existence. Companies in the same industry have often needed to enter into alliances to win in the long term and in automobiles, the case is all the more compelling. Tipu's life teaches us that the need to build alliances for long-term success is as important today as it was in his time.

Personal touch

Tipu's relevance is not just in the distant past. In the early days of my career in the auto industry, I met an absolutely brilliant R & D head—he had patents to his name and was a much sought-after speaker in technical conferences but was always of the opinion that his peers in quality and manufacturing did not know as much as he did. He never made the effort to educate them, share his passion the way they could understand it and build a rapport with them. At the end of meetings, he would go back feeling that they did not understand his brilliance, while his peers would go back saying he was too theoretical and fixated on a perfection that was impossible to achieve in a production environment. Sadly, the organisation never realised his potential completely and while he did achieve some fame, he had made little tangible impact to show for it. If he had built deeper connections and alliances with his immediate peers instead of conference organisers elsewhere, his legacy may have been richer.

What other lessons do you see from Tipu's life for today's corporate world?

Further Reading

Denys Forrest, *Tiger of Mysore: The Life and Death of Tipu Sultan* (Chatto and Windus, 1970)

John F. Riddick, *The History of British India: A Chronology* (Greenwood Publishing, 2006)

Lewin B. Bowring, *Rulers of India: Hyder Ali and Tipu Sultan* (S. Chand and Co., 1969)

SERFOJI II OF THANJAVUR

> *Serfoji II (1777–1832) was a Maratha king who ruled Thanjavur in Tamil Nadu. He came to power after a bitter succession struggle with the help of the East India Company. In return for their support, all of his military privileges and much of his kingdom was taken away. He was left with a generous pension and a town to rule over. Serfoji used his time and the money wisely and was an enlightened monarch. His list of achievements are varied and remarkable. What is even more noteworthy is that he chose to make an impact when he could have easily frittered away both his pension and his time.*

The Thanjavur Maratha kings

Utter the word 'Thanjavur' and everyone will talk of the Brihadeeswara temple and the Thanjavur style of paintings. Famous across India for the liberal use of gold foil and coloured glass stones, the creator of this painting genre teaches us a valuable lesson in leadership, though he is largely forgotten, even in his place of birth.

Thanjavur is a town and a district in Tamil Nadu watered by the Kaveri river. It is fertile and has played a pivotal role in the development of arts in southern India. Carnatic music and Bharatanatyam, as we know them today, were codified here. The region was first ruled by the Cholas, then occupied by the Pandyas and, after the invasions of the Delhi Sultanate, was occupied by the

Vijayanagara kings who ruled from Hampi in Karnataka. Their representative or Nayak ruled Thanjavur. When the Vijayanagar empire fell to the Bahmani Sultans, the stepbrother of Shivaji, Venkoji, captured Thanjavur and began the Maratha dynasty that lasted from 1674 to 1855.

By the eighteenth century, the Maratha kings had become vassals of the Nawab of Carnatic. The Nawab was heavily dependent on the East India Company that had by then become a powerful power in the region, having defeated the French. The then ruler of Thanjavur, Thuljaji (ruled in two spells from 1763–73 and 1776–87) had to cede much of his territory to the East India Company (and pay for an army to be stationed in his remaining territory as well).

Serfoji becomes the heir to the throne

Thuljaji had a small kingdom to rule and spent much of his time in the patronage of the arts. He also did not have a male heir. In 1787, he adopted a eleven-year-old boy who was a distant relative called Serfoji as his heir. A formal court or 'sadar' was held in the Thanjavur Palace and at the insistence of the German Missionary, Rev. Schwartz, and the British resident Huddlestone, Thuljaji rather reluctantly agreed to appoint his brother Amarasimha as the regent till Serfoji came of maturity. Thuljaji died soon after in the same year.

Serfoji's misfortunes before he became king

Amarasimha did everything possible to usurp the throne. He locked away the young boy in a dark room in the palace, denied him education and even proper food and allowed very few servants access to the boy. He bribed officers and Europeans to get them to declare that Serfoji's adoption was invalid. The East India Company Governor in Madras, Sir Archibald Campbell, was easily persuaded for he was keener on political stability in the region and preferred to support an adult king rather than get into the complexities of traditional Hindu law and stoke instability in the region, which would be counterproductive to the Company's revenues. Thuljaji's wives, however, were able to whip up enough protests for the governor to visit Thanjavur. Serfoji was represented by Rev. Schwartz and Amarasimha by twelve pandits. The latter had been bribed by Amarasimha and declared the adoption invalid. Schwartz had no knowledge of Hindu rules of adoption and had to agree.

Amarasimha became king and gave further concessions to the company but Rev. Schwartz and the queens weren't keeping quiet. Amarasimha's ill-treatment of Serfoji continued and the boy, with Schwartz, left Thanjavur and came to Madras. From 1792 to 1798, Schwartz and the queens relentlessly pursued Serfoji II's case. Schwartz's word as a European and an independent opinion from a set of pandits in Kashi given to the Governor General Lord Cornwallis, declaring Amarasimha's claim as invalid, helped. On 29 June 1798, supported by the East India Company, Amarsimha was dethroned and Serfoji II formally became the ruler.

Serfoji as king

The support of the British came at a price. The remaining part of the Thanjavur kingdom was taken away from Serfoji and he was allowed to rule only the fort, a small area of about 30 sq. kms. He received an annual grant of Rs 3.5 lakh and the entire army and land revenue system was taken over by the British. Serfoji could have now lived a life of leisure. He had the time to do whatever he wanted since he had no administrative responsibilities. He had the money to spend and no one to keep him in check. He, however, choose a different path and that is why he finds a place here. Rather than lead a life of disillusionment, waste his money on liquor and other vices, he chose, within his limited sphere, to be a role model leader for today, till his death in 1832.

His varied contributions

Education

In his time, educational institutions in India were either traditional ones that focussed exclusively on teaching the philosophical and religious texts open only to the upper castes or others run by missionaries that focussed on Western education designed to prepare students to take on clerical jobs with the administration. Serfoji, after his freedom from Amarasimha, had acquired a mix of both traditional education in Sanskrit, Marathi, Tamil and Telugu and was well-versed in Urdu, Dutch, Greek, Latin, German and English. He founded within the fort the Navavidya Kalanidhi Sala, a school for children that was an amalgam of Indian and Western education. It taught subjects in the arts, sciences, languages and also paid attention to knowledge derived from Western sources. In the four main streets around the fort, four Tamil-medium schools were begun.

The Maratha kings and queens had for long built chathrams (rest houses) alongside highways. Serfoji utilised this existing network of buildings and infrastructure that was now in East India Company territory but nominally belonged to him (as the King) to start schools. In the Muktambal Chatram alone, 436 students were given free boarding and lodging.

Serfoji also revolutionised the system by making education available to girls and encouraged them to attend by employing woman teachers. Serfoji was a voracious reader and frequently ordered books in several languages from abroad. Realising the need to teach creatively, he composed the *Devendra Kuravanji* in Marathi. The Kuravanji is an ancient genre where a well-travelled gypsy woman is asked by the heroine, to tell the latter's fortune, especially if the heroine will marry the man of her dreams. Serfoji changed the plot. He made Saraswati, the goddess of learning, the gypsy, edited out the fortune-telling part to a bare minimum and focussed on the part where the gypsy speaks of her travels. In a traditional Kuravanji, the travels are to famous pilgrim spots in Tamil Nadu. But in his work, the gypsy travels across several continents, in effect serving as a geography textbook. To address the issue of the lack of text books, he created his own printing press—a true example of not just complaining but doing something about it even if it meant going down the value chain to the basic inputs.

His biggest expenditure was towards the Sarasvati Mahal Library of Thanjavur that is named after him. The library has a huge collection of rare manuscripts. Books on water divining, food, elephant/horse training and maintenance share shelf space with books on astrology, astronomy, philosophy, literature and religion. The court records in the Modi script give us minute details of the palace and administration right down to the cost of vegetables that the kitchens consumed monthly to the diplomatic messages despatched to the French or British.

Medicine/health

Serfoji was deeply interested in medicine and was even open to learning dissection of cadavers, unthinkable for a man of his position and caste at that time. Court records show several lengthy correspondences with medical practitioners in Madras and London for him to obtain a model skeleton in ivory or wood that looked exactly like the real thing since he could not keep an actual skeleton. A skeleton model in wood was finally made and it was with him for many years. There are also meticulous records of his eye surgeries—with copious notes and illustrations of before and after as well as prescriptions and advice for patients. He compiled medicine prescription books, food recipes and health food recipes.

Other interests

His interests in shipbuilding had him construct a lighthouse in Manora on the Tamil Nadu coast and fund a small fleet of ships. He also created the genre of Tanjore paintings, started many more chathrams, enlarged their services to the local community, maintained a zoo and lavishly supported temples, poets, dramatists and charities.

Life lessons

Serfoji's treatment by Amarasimha as a child, the heavy price the British extracted to put him back on the throne, the low pension he received (how much of money is ever enough for anyone!) and many other mishaps could have led Serfoji down the path of self-pity and lamentation. However, he choose to step out of the circle of concern and into a smaller circle of control, and focussed on what he could make of the situation that he was in. All of us have this option every time we complain. Closer in connection are serial entrepreneurs who even after selling off their company choose to start new ventures and build new value rather than just sitting back and relaxing. The new ideas continue to employ people, serve customer needs and add value to the community at large.

The business connection

As a consultant, I have had the good fortune of spending many hours with very senior leaders across India. One thing I have found common among them is they seldom, if ever, complain about the outside world. They do not complain about the market or competition or the policies and even if they did, it would be a casual remark quickly moving on to what can be done about it.

Great leaders are also great problem-solvers—either problems they were facing at that moment or those they think will occur in the future. With their focus on things like these, they have no energy to complain but get on with fixing things as best as they could. In having this attitude, they were similar to Serfoji II.

Personal touch

Thanjavur has fascinated me for as long as I can remember and I have written two books on the city. When I was racing against time to complete my second manuscript, on many occasions when I was stuck in traffic jams in Bangalore (where I was living then) or waiting for delayed flights, it was much more efficient to turn on the laptop and get going with the manuscript, rather than sit back and complain. Serfoji, of course, did this at a bigger scale, but if we listed out our complaints, I am sure for many of them, we can move from being concerned to actually controlling what we can do. Typing instead of complaining about the traffic jam or flight delay may seem like a small activity but it saved me many hours and that was a lot in a time when I was always doing more things than I had time for.

Conclusion

It is easy to play victim and complain about how things ought to be. However, those who have left a mark on the world chose to act to either overcome their limitations or find ways to circumvent them.

Whether in Serfoji II's time or in the lives of anyone who has achieved impact, success has come to those who worked within their limitations and stretched them rather than adopting a defeatist attitude. As we increase our circle of control and reduce our circle of concerns, there is a greater chance we can live into our fullest potential.

Further Reading

Tulajendra Rajah P. Bhosale, *Rajah Serfoji II With a Short History of the Thanjavur Mahrattas* (T.R.P. Bhosale, 1995)

Pradeep Chakravarthy and Vikram Sathyanathan, *Thanjavur: A Cultural History* (Niyogi Books, 2010)

Savithri Preetha Nair, *Raja Serfoji II: Science, Medicine and Enlightenment in Tanjore* (Routledge Taylor and Francis Group, 2012)

K.M. Venkataramayya, *Thanjai Marathia Mannarkaala Arasiyalum Samuthaya Vazhkaiyum* (Thanjavur Tamil University, 1984)

B. Madhu Gopal, 'Anatomy and history of a 200-year-old ivory skeleton', 6 April 2018, *The Hindu*, https://www.thehindu.com/news/national/andhra-pradesh/anatomy-and-history-of-a-200-year-old-ivory-skeleton/article23448299.ece

Chronicles of the East

SANKARADEVA

> *Sankaradeva (1449–1568) was a saint, scholar, poet and religious reformer of Assam. His compositions continue to be popular and the satras or monasteries he established are an important feature of Assam's religious landscape. He is deeply revered in Assam even today and his role in religious reform and giving access to ancient texts to the larger population is widely remembered.*

Assam before Sankaradeva

The Brahmaputra valley that comprises Assam, Bhutan and parts of Bengal were in the old days known as Kamarupa. The original inhabitants were known as Kiratas or hunters and there were many small kingdoms like the Khens, Koch, Kachari and others that rose and fell in the region. The kingdom of the Ahoms was formed in the eleventh century. The Ahoms were a group who came from South China, but they very quickly integrated with the local population and absorbed their culture. By the sixteenth century, they had created a powerful kingdom and were even able to fight victoriously against the Mughals.

Sankaradeva's contribution was towards the cultural unification of the region. During the first half of the second millennium in India, there were multiple factors that led to the development of new dimensions in Hinduism. These were largely based on the Bhakti doctrine, and several saints in various parts of the country were exponents of this liberal and progressive movement that preached a faith based on constant devotion, stood against excessive ritualism, caste prejudices and stressed on the equality of all.

In Sankaradeva's time, society was sharply divided on caste lines and several parts of Hindu philosophical thought like the Upanishads were kept away from the majority of the population. This was caused by and worsened by political instability. The minor kingdoms of the Assam region had not been fully absorbed by the Ahoms and there was bitter rivalry. Also, internal succession struggles within each kingdom left the region in a state of confusion.

Assam had long been a place for Shakta worship—the worship of Parvati as the primary Goddess was the practice and the Kamakhya temple was (and still is) an important pilgrimage site. During that time, Shakta worship combined tantric traditions that emphasised heavily on esoteric rituals, mantras and sacrifices.

A brief account of his life

Sankaradeva was born into the Baro-Bhuyan clan near Bordowa in present-day Nagaon district in 1449. They were warrior chiefs and zamindars in Assam. Due to the untimely death of his parents at a very early age, Sankaradeva was brought up by his grandmother.

His grandmother enrolled him in a 'tol' (school) run by a Sanskrit pandit at the age of twelve. His first work, *Harishchandra Upakhyana*, was written while at the tol. In 1465, upon mastering the texts taught at the school, he married and assumed his position as the leader of his clan.

The death of his wife prompted him to go on a pilgrimage to the major centres of the Vaishnava religion of that time—Puri, Gaya, Ayodhya, Sitakunda, Vrindavan, Mathura, Badrinath, Dwaraka and Rameswaram. It is possible, in these places, he would have been more fully exposed to the ideas and songs of the Bhakti movement. In Puri, he came into contact with many scholars with whom he interacted. This sparked off the initial thoughts behind what later became the neo-Vaishnavisim movement in Assam.

On his return, Sankaradeva established a small temple and continued his scholarly explorations, when he was given a copy of the Bhagavatha Purana. This text celebrates Krishna and says that the path to him is in reciting his name in groups. Sankaradeva took it upon himself to propagate this path in the region. Threats of political invasion caused him to move places until he settled in the Ahom kingdom and began translating the entire Bhagavata Purana from Sanskrit to Assamese so that common people could understand it better. Translation of Sanskrit scriptures to vernacular languages so that it could be easily understood by common people was one of the important steps taken by the Bhakti figures.

Further invasions forced Sankaradeva to move to Dhuwahat (that has since been washed away by the Brahmaputra) where the numbers of his followers swelled. One of his important followers was Madhavadeva, who would go on to become a driving force behind the advancement of Vaishnavism in Assam.

Sankaradeva preached an easier path to Krishna that did not need idols, expensive rituals or even knowledge of Sanskrit. This was not to the liking of the orthodox. He constructed kirtanghar or prayer halls for devotees to sing and chant. All the different groups of the region were treated as one in these kirtanghar. The King of Cooch Behar became his devotee after he won a debate with other scholars and that helped him establish a base in the kingdom. Meanwhile, he continued his translation of the Bhagavata Purana.

Sankaradeva frequented the Cooch capital for more than twenty years and enjoyed continuous royal patronage till his death in 1568.

Life lessons

During Sankaradeva's time, Assam was divided politically by kingdoms and socially by caste and there was a lot of chaos and confusion in the life of people. To remedy this aspect of society, his teachings were about healing and bringing people together by promoting a common cultural, social and economic vision using religion and philosophy.

His writings emphasised on the moral, ethical and spiritual aspects of religion. Drawing from the epics and the Puranas, he extolled and elaborated on the merits of virtues such as truth, mercy and forgiveness, charity, non-violence, absence of envy and jealousy, patience, respect and control of the senses. In his teachings, the vices that lead to misery, destruction and to an unspiritual life were sensual pleasure, anger, desire, delusion, pride, envy and jealousy. In placing the focus on the core, he preached against any practices—superstitions or rituals—that deviated from this.

Mass appeal

In Sankaradeva's time, the core texts, especially the Bhagavatha Purana, were in Sanskrit that was not spoken or understood by the majority of the common people. In translating it into the local language and using Assamese for his major writings, songs, verses and plays, Sankaradeva democratised access to the texts and its philosophy to those who did not know Sanskrit. Through literature, drama, poetry, songs, dance and music, he unified and uplifted an entire community. The use of music and plays to promote philosophy was a wonderful innovation. They were not only easy to grasp but provided entertainment as well. In a way, he made learning fun!

His Borgeets set to classical tunes are sung even today by all sorts of people. Another contribution of his is the 'Ankiya-Bhaona' or performances that blend music, dance, discourse and recitation according to the orthodox Natyashastra style. Sankaradeva created dance-dramas like the *Cihna yatra*, for which he painted the Sapta Vaikuntha (seven heavens), helped make the musical instruments and played them himself.

He also engaged the weavers of Tantikuchi, near Barpeta, to weave a forty-yard long tapestry of the images of childhood of Lord Krishna in Vrindavan. Sankaradeva personally provided the designs to be woven, chose the various colours of thread to be used, and supervised the weaving. It took about a year to complete and came to be known as the 'Vrindavana Vastra'. A section of this cloth is at the Victoria and Albert Museum in London. Visual representations like this are effective visual aids and would have been very useful in reaching out to those who may not have been able to read.

Thus, Sankaradeva's activities raised the level of social ethics and enriched the cultural fabric, thereby widening the intellectual and imaginative horizon of the common mind.

Royal patronage

At a time when kings were the most powerful men in the region and when there were frequent clashes between neighbouring kings, Sankaradeva needed the support of kings for his own safety and for his message to be spread without obstruction.

He seems to have been a charismatic leader able to win over kings through his scholarship and ingenuity. His debating skills won him the support of the two main rulers in the region, the Ahom ruler, Suhungmuhung, and the Cooch King, Naranarayana. The latter even wished to become a full-time disciple but Sankaradeva refused, saying that being a full-time disciple would come at the cost of performing his duties as a king.

His many talents also seemed to have helped in earning him

respect. When Naranarayana asked the court poets to write a condensed version of the entire twelve cantos of the Bhagavata Purana, Sankaradeva took up the challenge and accomplished the feat in one night and prepared the 'Gunamala Puthi', which he put it into a small wooden box. Then over this, he painted with hengul-haital (yellow and red colours) an elephant squeezed inside a circle. He called it Bhurukaat Haathi, meaning an elephant squeezed into a lime-pot. The Puthi was placed in the sanctum sanatorum of the prayer hall, instead of the idol and worshipped as the Chaitanya.

His ability to translate the concept of equality into action

Sankaradeva's institutionalising the message of equality was vital to his success. The Naamghar, the most important institution which Sankaradeva gave to Assam, is even today run on democratic principles, with all villagers having a voice and hand in its management. Not only are its doors open to all but all villagers, irrespective of their caste and race, are also allowed to participate in its cultural activities and the Naamacharya can be from any caste. Similarly, the Deuri (person who distributes prasad offerings) and the artistes in Ankiya Naat and Gayan-Bayan are selected on the basis of their religious attainments and aptitude rather than their social backgrounds.

Sankaradeva raised socially downtrodden communities to the level of the higher castes by installing them as 'bhakats' (devotees) and 'mahantas' (noble men). The first to be initiated was the wife of a leper, others were a tantric, a trader, Brahmins, an ascetic, and members from communities like the Garo, Jaintia, Bhutia, Koch and even a Muslim. His patient, persistent nature and his persuasive style and accurate interpretation convinced even those who opposed him initially to support him later.

The business connection

Sankaradeva comes across as a powerful persuader. In all his messages, the underlining need he seems to be stressing to those who believed in him was that they are worthy of respect and their connection to a higher God need not be through intermediaries. Making them feel worthy of self-respect by themselves and respect from others is an important aspect of his legacy. How he did this is also interesting. He used music and images. Music tugs at the emotional hearts of the people and in singing as a group, the connection to the other and, therefore, to oneself is powerfully reached. This is a core Indian concept originating from the way our thoughts and feelings were organised in the early river valley economy, where for rice cultivation, one needed the others much more than the others needed them. The words, the melody and the act of singing together powerfully excite the emotional connect and, therefore, the intellectual connect as well and from that not only is self-respect increased but also a sense of social connection, which is another fundamental need of human beings. Using the common language is another subtle but powerful tool.

'A picture speaks a thousand words' is something we have often heard. In creating the Vrindavana Vastra, Sankaradeva was using images to tell a story and in giving a visual for his music and voice, he was making the persuasion much more compelling, just the way powerfully made slides and films can be inspirational in today's world.

In the Sankaradeva story, that he undermined the importance of rituals is important. Similarly, are there beliefs and behaviours that we too doggedly hold on to? These are the rituals that prevent us from attaining our potential.

Organisations too have many rituals. The performance appraisal system in many organisations is a ritual that is complied with rather than committed to. It is in our nature to want predictability and to slowly become set in the way we think, speak and act. When that happens, everything becomes a ritual that gives us comfort and security. When they are not examined and altered, we as individuals or as organisations run the risk of becoming obsolete.

In the corporate world, there are many examples of leaders who have left a lasting legacy because they have worked towards earning the respect of others and connected to them emotionally. There have also been leaders who have constantly looked at how rituals in their organisations need to be changed or removed altogether and substituted them with new ones, if necessary.

Just as Sankaradeva used art and music to connect with people, using social media creatively to build brand image has been done effectively by modern-day leaders.

Leaders who are active on social media have several million followers and have been able to forge a connect with Gen X and beyond. Sankaradeva interestingly used music and images for his long-lasting legacy. He realised the persuasive capacity of the arts just as modern leaders have to use social media for persuasively and emotionally establishing a connection with the brand.

Conclusion

Sankaradeva, with his clear vision and creative ways of persuasion, altered the society to become more value-driven and inclusive. His stress on equality and his use of the creative arts to communicate his message are lasting legacies indeed.

Further Reading

Maheshwar Neog, *Sankaradeva and his Times: Early History of the Vaishnava Faith and Movement in Assam* (Motilal Banarsidass, 2nd Edition, 1980)

Maheshwar Neog, *Cultural Heritage of Assam* (Omsons Publishers, 2008)

Lakshminath Bezbaroa, 'History of Vaishnavism in India', http://www.atributetosankaradeva.org/History_of_Vaisnavism.pdf

A Creative Vision: Essays on Sankaradeva and Neo-Vaisnava Movement in Assam (Srimanta Sankar Kristi Bikash Samiti, 2004)

Dimbeswar Neog, *Jagatguru Sankaradeva, the Founder of Mahapurusism* (Srimanta Sankaradeva Sangha, 1963)

http://atributetosankaradeva.org/main.htm

THE AHOMS OF ASSAM

The Ahoms entered the Brahmaputra Valley in present-day Assam from north Myanmar and established their supremacy in 1228 CE under their leader Chaolung Sukaphaa. The word 'Ahom' is derived from the word 'Asama', meaning invincible, a local name for this mighty tribe that ruled for over 600 years. The Ahoms consolidated the entire valley into one empire and ruled until they were defeated by the British in 1826.

Historical accounts suggest that when the Ahoms entered, the region was thinly populated. Sukhapha befriended the local groups, the Barahi and the Marans, and established his capital at Charaideo. The Ahom kingdom was based on the Paik system, a type of labour wherein farmers also performed soldiering duties during times of war.

The Ahoms introduced wet rice cultivation in upper Assam that was largely a marshy and thinly populated land. Rice cultivation coupled with reclamation of land using dykes, embankments and irrigation systems helped the Ahoms establish themselves and create the initial state structures. The locals who took to the Ahom way of life and polity were incorporated into their fold. As a result, the number of people who came to be regarded as Ahoms grew significantly and by the sixteenth century under Suhungmung, they made territorial expansions at the cost of the Chutiya and Kachari kingdoms. As the Ahoms continued to push west, conflict with the Mughals and their allies was only a matter of time.

> *With the conquest of Bengal in 1576, the Mughals had the opportunity to expand their empire to the Northeast, particularly into the Koch kingdom and into Assam. With this goal in mind, they marched through these regions in the beginning of the seventeenth century. Besides the urge to conquer more territory, the plentiful supply of elephants in the region would have been an additional incentive, as the Mughals used elephants for warfare, transportation services and as a symbol of power.*

The Mughals and the Ahoms

The Ahoms' resistance to the Mughals spanned from 1615 to 1682. Till the end, the Mughals were never able to completely defeat the Ahoms. In 1639, during the reign of Shah Jahan, a Treaty of Peace was signed between Ahom general Momai Tamuli Borbarua and Mughal commander Allah Yar Khan. According to the treaty, western Assam commencing from Guwahati was to be ceded to the Mughals and all territories east of river Barnadi in the north and Kalang on the south of Brahmaputra continued to stay under the control of the Ahoms. This treaty came after a protracted conflict which the Ahoms conducted very strategically. They initially consolidated their armies and attempted to buy time by making peace proposals and promising consignments of elephants for the army and a regular supply of aloes wood that was used for making incense for the Mughal court. The war, when it was finally fought, ended in a stalemate that resulted in the signing of a treaty.

In 1661, Aurangzeb who pursued a more expansionist strategy ordered the Mughal governor of Bengal, Mir Jumla, to invade Assam. By March 1662, Mir Jumla had occupied large parts of the Ahom kingdom, including Guwahati and Garhgaon. But his victory was short-lived. He found it difficult to cross the hilly terrain. Also, the Ahom forts were strong and their warriors courageous. The early onset of the monsoon and regular night raids also weakened Mir Jumla. Mir Jumla was compelled to sign the Treaty of Ghilajharighat in 1663 with the Ahom king Jayadhwaj Singha who agreed to pay a huge war indemnity. The terms of the treaty were highly in favour of the Mughals. Mir Jumla then retreated to Dhaka, the army troubled by storms and lack of food and he himself passed away on his way back in March 1663. Chakradhwaj Singha succeeded Jayadhwaj Singha in 1663 and resolved to free the country from the heavy indemnity payable to the Mughal emperor. He raised an army and prepared to attack the Mughals.

Within five years, the Ahoms took back control of most of the lost territories. In August 1667, the Ahom General Lachit, who was given the title Borphukan or commander, recovered possession of Guwahati. This enraged Aurangzeb and in December 1667 he tasked Raja Ram Singh of Amer with invading Assam in what would be the last Mughal attempt to conquer this region. In February 1669, Raja Ram Singh reached Rangamati with a large force to conquer Assam.

Raja Ram Singh entered Assam via Rangamati with 4,000 troopers, 500 imperial gunners, 30,000 infantries, forces of 21 Rajput chiefs and 40 war boats. At Cooch Behar, he was joined by 15,000 archers and infantry. The army cavalry was large, numbering around 20,000. The Ahoms were vastly outnumbered.

It was in this situation that Lachit Borphukan showed his tactical brilliance. Being well aware of the fact that the Ahoms wouldn't stand a chance at winning an open plain battle, Lachit Borphukan chose to engage with the Mughals in Guwahati owing to its hilly terrain. The only way to get to Guwahati from the east was via the Brahmaputra river. So, he set up a naval defence at Saraighat where the Brahmaputra was at its narrowest and then retreated to Guwahati. At Guwahati, the fortifications were created in a way that they could defend fiercely and also force the Mughals to take the river route. Borphukan's tactics of guerrilla attacks severely demoralised the ill-prepared Mughal forces.

There were further battles between the two opposing forces before things came to a head at the Battle of Saraighat in 1671. The Ahoms emerged victorious in this battle. This battle is immortalised in Assamese literature and today, one can visit the village called Sarai on the banks of Brahmaputra and get a glimpse of what transpired.

It was the last major attempt by the Mughals to extend their empire into Assam. Aurangzeb's successors could never launch any further effective expeditions against the Ahoms. Though the Mughals managed to regain Guwahati briefly later on, the Ahoms wrested control in the Battle of Itakhuli in 1682 and put a stop to the Mughal expansion in Assam.

The Ahoms were never conquered by the mighty Mughal army and their clever strategic warfare tactics and intuitive use of terrain and geographic conditions helped them inflict one of the worst defeats in the history of the Mughals.

The business connection

The ability of the Ahoms to capture and retain a kingdom for about 600 years is a lesson in continuity. What did they do right? They were, of course, lucky enough to have geographical boundaries that made it difficult for outsiders to invade them. But some of their other decisions worked to ensure their long reign. They were able to give an assured food supply for their people through the introduction of rice cultivation that they brought with them from south east Asia. In the business context, that would mean constantly looking at the landscape around you and sensing change and being nimble to it. In the past, it can be seen in the traders, especially Jains who came from Rajasthan to Bengal and how they adapted to the Mughals and then to the British. It meant a geographical shift from Dhaka to Murshidabad and then to Kolkata as the Mughal rule gave way to the local Nawabs and eventually the British. They were moneylenders and then traders and they were willing to change their base and the business to continue to survive. In an organisation I worked with the father and then the son, I could see their willingness to constantly look at new opportunities and partnerships and have no sentiment in closing and exiting business if they did not work out in the long run, and the owners were convinced that they had done their best but it would not work. The father admitted that it was a tough choice to exit the older textile business that they had originally started out with to move into newer energy sectors and he admitted that he had heated arguments with his son. He confided, 'Well, we had many long, sometimes heated arguments, but at the end of the day, I had to admit that the old business I had started was not where my son's passions lay and for our sectors the margins were difficult so it was easier to change when we had a choice than to be forced into it. How can we be sentimental about such things?' The old man did admit that his son would make mistakes but would learn from them. 'After all, I did too and that was what made the textile trading business grow, hopefully he won't make the same ones but I am sure he will learn how to adapt and survive.' As time has changed, the solar energy business is steadily growing and the textile trading business continues but only in token form but is still profitable.

The other connection to learn from is the strategy-making of Lachit. He was a quick thinker, nimble enough to use the terrain and able to quickly change tactics, which the larger and more rigid Mughal army could not. His example, as others in this book, is a reminder of a common lesson from many historic battles—the larger, more hierarchical armies have a tendency to become rigid, are less responsive to quickly changing situations and, therefore, often lose to smaller, agile and more flexible armies. The connection here is to larger companies or even older people becoming more rigid about change.

Companies must also note the importance of control. Before businesses consider growing, they should have processes in place to have effective controls. This means obtaining reliable information, being aware of the significance and uses of that information and developing the capacity to identify and resolve problems before they become deep-seated.

Conclusion

The history of the Ahoms and the masterful strategy of Lachit are valuable lessons for us in two ways. Their ability to be nimble, responsive and persistent are all qualities much needed in our lives today. The pandemic and the disruption it has caused has taught us how much more it is important to not take things for granted. On the other side, it also teaches us the danger of having a set and rigid point of view that translates into many and complex processes that hinder us from changing fast. The tendency when one comes across a statement like the previous one is to find fault with our organisations' processes—say, the billing process or the approval process. That may well be true but it is not just that. The rigidity within our own minds of 'things should be done only this way', 'I know whatever I need to know' and other such statements that we make when faced with a choice, are just as dangerous and make it all the more important for us to learn from the Ahoms and Lachit.

Further Reading

S.L. Baruah, *A Comprehensive History of Assam* (Munshiram Manoharlal Publishers, 1985)

E. Gait, *A History of Assam* (EBH Publishers, Indian Reprint, 2008)

N. Nath, *History of the Koch Kingdom, c. 1515-1615* (Mittal Publications, 1989)

D. Sahariah, D. & T. Halder, 'Revisiting Koch-Mughal Relations: A Political History from Alliance to Disintegration', *Asian Journal of Multidisciplinary Studies*, Vol. 4, Issue 1, January 2016

Jadunath Sarkar, *History of Aurangzeb. Vol III* (M.C. Sarkar & Sons, 1921)

Leaders Who Did Not Enlarge their Legacy

'Bad' and 'good' are very value-laden terms. They will vary with time, place and person and are very individual points of view. In the context of leadership, they can be very contextual as well. However, an essential part of leadership is the leaving of a legacy that is appreciated by those who come after and in enriching and building on what is already there. In this expectation, we can learn from the errors of the last Nizam of Hyderabad and the Mughals who succeeded Aurangzeb. The point is not to paint them as 'good' or 'bad' but to only understand what they did or did not do in growing their kingdom and, therefore, leaving a positive legacy.

OSMAN ALI KHAN OF HYDERABAD

In 1911, one of the largest princely states in British India welcomed a new ruler. Osman Ali Khan was the seventh Nizam of Hyderabad. Hyderabad state had been established in the eighteenth century by Nizam Ul-Mulk Asaf Jha following the break-up of the Mughal Empire.

Osman Ali Khan inherited a state larger than more than twenty of the original UN signatories, as Winston Churchill put it. His private wealth was immeasurable. He would be, in 1937, the richest man in the world and would appear on the cover of Time magazine at the time of his silver jubilee that same year. However, private wealth could not ensure that he always got his way, and he would be forced to give up his throne, accede to India and accept a reduced status before the end of his life.

Post the merger of Hyderabad with India, Osman Ali Khan was retained as the governor of Hyderabad. He continued to retain possession of his palaces, lived off his immeasurable wealth, himself maintained a frugal lifestyle, but supported many of relatives, as well as many children, none of whom were equipped to live ordinary lives. He was removed from his position in 1956 when India was reorganised on a linguistic basis, and Hyderabad state was reorganised into Andhra Pradesh. However, he retained his palaces, and his annual contributions and scholarships contributed to institutions like Osmania University and several others continued.

In 1967, the Nizam passed away at the age of eighty.

Hyderabad at the time of Indian independence

When India gained independence, Osman Ali Khan was not in favour of joining the Indian Union. Hyderabad was surrounded by British India, with Madras Presidency to its south and east, the Bombay Presidency to its west and the Central Provinces to the north. It was a state ruled by a Muslim family but the majority of whose subjects were Hindu. Most historians are of the view that most of Hyderabad's subjects at that time wished to join India.

In 1927, an organisation known as the Majlis Ittehad Ul-Muslimeen (MIM) had been founded. The leader of the MIM at the time of Independence was Kasim Rizvi, a man with a strong belief in the independence of Hyderabad, who urged the Nizam to retain sovereignty. Rizvi had also created a paramilitary force in the state—the Razakars.

The Nizam had expected the support of the British, especially as he had supported all their endeavours, against the word of other Muslim leaders. Now, they officially stated that princely states had the options as stated in the Instrument of Accession, and they would not give them any other support, no matter the nature of their past dealings. In 1946, the Nizam stated that he was going to stay independent, expecting that his wealth could sustain the nation independently for some time and hoping that he could convince the British to back him up. This was not something the newly-formed government of independent India was agreeable to. After attempting to resolve the situation through diplomacy, in September 1948, the Indian Army occupied Hyderabad in just three days. The Nizam's rule was at an end.

Why could the Nizam not continue to be independent?

The Nizam's riches were legendary, and he was a man, who, in one anecdote, was supposed to have used a diamond as a paperweight. Yet, these riches could not secure him from merger with the state of India. Here are a few reasons why:

The support of the people was not completely with his government

Hyderabad state was not as prosperous as the Nizam himself. Though the richest man in the world, he was known for his stinginess and tightfistedness, even towards himself. Though he won some praise for his handling of the Great Depression in the Thirties, his state was largely poverty-stricken. From 1946, Muslims from the surrounding regions flocked to the state, and many Hindus fled to Madras, amid rising tensions and Hyderabad's announcement about remaining independent. During the last few years of Hyderabad's resistance, the Congress, which had been petitioning through the Forties for increased representative governance, began increased demands for the merger of Hyderabad. With the support of grassroots workers and the public, they organised further protests and demonstrations. Many were jailed. But they demonstrated that the people of the state were with them. Meanwhile, the Communist Party held protests and marches of their own in the rural areas, seizing land holdings over 500 acres and redistributing them. Slowly, they worked their way down until holdings over 100 acres no longer existed. Forced labour was abolished by the communists. The Communist Party was temporarily banned. On 15 August 1947, across Hyderabad, the Indian tricolour was hoisted by the Congress. Those who took part in hoisting the Indian flag were arrested.

The people's support was not always with the Nizam. His government was supported by the Razakars and the MIM, who were intensely pro-Muslim. This only acted to polarise Hyderabad, and did nothing to soothe tensions.

The firmness of India and the conviction of Sardar Patel

The Indian state was firm in its decision that it would assimilate all princely states into the federation. This meant that there was no way they would tolerate an independent nation virtually in the centre of the country. Patel worked round the clock, visiting states, promising rulers privy purses, or positions of power in the Indian state, and getting them to sign the Instrument of Accession. At times, Mountbatten who had been appointed Governor-General, would also provide the final touches. The Nizam, however, was firm. Nothing was going to sway him. The MIM was opposed to democracy, and he did not want to give up the independence of his state. Right until the end, he stood his ground, until India had no choice but to send in the army, over a year after Independence.

Military power mismatch

Hyderabad did not have the military strength to withstand the Indian army, and the Nizam knew it. However, egged on by the Razakars, the Nizam decided to go ahead and refuse to budge on his independent status. He did make attempts to bolster his military and, as a last ditch effort, lifted the ban on the Communist Party in the hopes that the peasants, led by the communists, would resist the Indian army. But it was a case of too little, too late.

On 13 September 1948, the Indian army invaded Hyderabad in a military mission titled 'Operation Polo'. Within three days, Hyderabad had been overrun, and though the Razakars and the army attempted to resist the Indian army, they did not have the numbers and their maps and weapons were outdated. Pakistan's help had been enlisted, but the death of Jinnah on 11 September ruled out any aid from them. They were easily defeated.

That is not to say that the takeover was simple. The military committed a series of atrocities on the state of Hyderabad upon entering it, the reports of which were not publicised at the time, and even now, are not very well known.

Life lessons

The Nizam's story is a lesson in how a leader put his own needs over that of his people. His country could not be financially viable and in the rising surge of nationalist feelings, the people were in favour of union with India. In this emotional issue, he was out of touch with his people and choose to go with his financial calculations and wealth instead of the feelings of his subjects. In all decisions we take, there is a trade-off between thoughts and feelings. In his case here, he operated from thoughts, while his people operated from feelings. Consulting research says that more than 70 per cent of change programmes across organisations, irrespective of geography, industry or holding pattern, fail not because of a want of bright ideas and well-thought-through plans but because the people involved don't 'buy in' and connect emotionally. They don't see a compelling reason to change and change 'now'.

Personal touch

In working with a first-generation entrepreneur, I have seen how passionately and strategically he viewed his organisation. This made him often think far ahead of the team, who were bewildered by the pace of change. For the leader, every day was a battle. But for the team, it was as if the leader didn't care or wasn't listening. They reacted by freezing at their tasks and then leaving when things became difficult. It was only after much introspection that the leader began to acknowledge that the feelings of his team were not always similar to his. Even more difficult was for him to find the right balance of listening and acting on the feelings of his team and, at the same time, taking the risks he needed to, for his company to navigate and thrive in a volatile and fiercely competitive market. The key lay in taking decisions jointly and communicating more and more deeply and frequently, neither of which the Nizam did.

THE MUGHALS AFTER AURANGZEB

Aurangzeb was succeeded by his eldest son Muhammad Mu'azzam, who took the name Bahadur Shah I (1707–12). He was sixty-three years old when he ascended the throne and had to fight off his brothers' claims. The situation was complicated since Aurangzeb himself did not have a harmonious relationship with his sons and distrusted them. The Rajputs and Sikhs were all simmering under the control of Aurangzeb and used this confusion to assert their independence.

The Marathas had long posed a serious challenge to the Mughals in the Deccan. Bahadur Shah installed Shahu, who was under Mughal captivity since 1689, as the raja of Satara with the view to pacifying the Marathas. He, in turn, appointed Balaji Visvanath as the Peshwa. His son Baji Rao would emerge as the greatest challenger of the Mughals later on.

Bahadur Shah's reign was short and he died in Lahore on 27 February 1712. His death was immediately followed by a new war of succession among his four sons. Three of them perished and Jahandar Shah secured the throne in 1712 with the help of Zulfiqar Khan, a powerful noble. He ruled only for a year. Zulfiqar soon turned traitor, captured the king by deception and presented him to Farrukhsiyar, Jahandar's cousin. Jahandar was put in prison and a few days later strangled to death by executioners.

Farrukhsiyar, the new emperor, ruled from 1713 to 1719. At that time, the Sikhs under their leader Banda Singh Bahadur were on the rise. Bahadur Shah had tried unsuccessfully to capture and kill Banda Singh. This time around, after an eight-month siege by the Mughal Army, the Sikhs surrendered in December 1715. Banda was taken to Delhi and put to death the following year. Farrukhsiyar had relied on the Sayyid brothers—Hussain Ali, the deputy governor of Patna, and Hasan Ali, the governor of Allahabad, to come to power and continued to lean on them once on the throne. The Sayyid brothers were appointed as the Wazir of the State and the commander of the army, respectively. Very soon, they took complete advantage of the situation. Farrukhsiyar made many attempts to get rid of them but in February 1719, in a palace coup of sorts, the Sayyid brothers imprisoned the emperor. Two months later, he was strangled to death. The Sayyid brothers placed the dead emperor's cousin Rafi-ud-Darajat on the throne in 1719. He died in few months. Rafi-ud-Daula succeeded him and he too died in four months. The Sayyid brothers then chose Raushan Akhtar to be the emperor.

Raushan Akhtar was Bahadur Shah's grandson. He ruled as Muhammad Shah from 1719 to 1748. He was eighteen years old when he came to the peacock throne. The Mughal army and, particularly, the Mughal artillery were still a force to reckon with. Administration in northern India had deteriorated but not broken down yet. But Muhammad Shah neglected the affairs of the state and lived a life of ease and luxury. He came to be known as a pleasure-loving ruler and was known as Muhammad Shah 'Rangila' (meaning colourful, an uncomplimentary reference to his debauchery). Nizam-ul-Mulk, the most powerful noble of the time, unhappy with the emperor, chose to go his own way. Appointed as the Wazir in 1722, he relinquished his office in 1724 and went on to establish the independent kingdom of Hyderabad.

In 1738-39, the Persian emperor Nadir Shah descended upon northern India. He occupied Lahore to begin with. Hurried preparations were made for Delhi's defence but the faction-ridden nobles refused to unite even in the sight of the enemy. Nadir Shah attacked and looted Delhi. His neglect of the army and administration made it impossible for him to withstand the might of Nadir Shah. This invasion sped up the disintegration of the Mughal Empire.

The rulers who came after Muhammad Shah were Ahmed Shah (1748–54); Alamgir II (1754–59); Shah Alam II, also known as Ali Guhar (1759–1806); Akbar II (1806–37) and Bahadur Shah II (1837–62).

Ahmed Shah (1748–54) was deposed by the Marathas and their allies in 1754. Thereafter, he lived in confinement until his death. Over the next few years, the Marathas extended their influence up to Delhi. In 1757, during Alamgir II's rule (1754–59), the East India Company fought the Battle of Plassey and defeated Siraj-ud-Daulah, the Nawab of Bengal, and got a foothold in Bengal. The East India Company began to slowly eat into the Mughal territory. After their defeat in the third battle of Panipat, the Marathas retreated to the Deccan and much of the Mughal empire that was left came to be controlled by the East India Company. In 1765, Shah Alam II granted the Dewani of Bengal, Bihar and Orissa to the East India Company, which allowed them to collect revenues from these areas. Akbar Shah II held the title from 1806 to 1837. He exercised very little power due to the increasing British control of India through the East India Company.

The eldest son of Emperor Akbar Shah II, Bahadur Shah II ('Zafar') was the last of the Mughal emperors in India. When he came to the throne in 1837, his rule extended only to Delhi and its surroundings. He held a purely symbolic and titular role, while the East India Company exercised real power. As the Indian rebellion of 1857 spread, the Indian regiments seized Delhi and proclaim Zafar their nominal head. As a result of reluctantly lending his name to the revolt of 1857, he was tried for treason by the British and exiled to Rangoon, Burma, in 1858 along with his wife Zeenat Mahal and some other family members.

To describe Bahadur Shah as weak would be unfair, as no Mughal had exercised real power since Alamgir II. Within the limited domain of Delhi's social life, however, Bahadur Shah did preside over a period of flourishing cultural life. 'Zafar' was his nom de plume as an Urdu poet. He was not only a mystical poet but also a calligrapher, theologian, creator of gardens and patron of miniature painters.

Life lessons from the later Mughals

While the Mughal empire reached its greatest extent under Aurangzeb's rule, it also declined swiftly within a few decades after his death. A combination of factors can be attributed to the decline of the Mughal empire.

The vast area that the Mughal empire covered by the end of Aurangzeb's rule had become impossible for one ruler to control. He facilitated its decline by leaving an overstretched empire with too many disgruntled subjects to his successors. During the reign of the later Mughals, the Deccan, Bengal, Bihar and Orissa declared their independence. The raids by Nadir Shah further weakened the empire. The consequent encroachment by the British and the French proved to be the last nail in the coffin.

The business connection

The organisation parallel is the founder entrepreneur not clearly demarcating roles for his children (or grandchildren). In many cases, it is an emotional decision to decide to give more power and control to one child, which, in turn, means the other is not 'good enough'. However, if the principle of equality is followed and every child is given a place in the running of the organisation, and merit takes a backseat, the performance of the organisation is likely to suffer. Family members may not necessarily be competent and there could be a demotivation among younger, brighter performers who see all the senior positions being filled only by members of the family.

The other factor that aided the decline was that Aurangzeb did not consolidate the empire in the sense of succession. As the Mughals did not follow a law of succession such as the law of primogeniture, it weakened the empire. His death signalled the outbreak of a war among his sons. Bahadur Shah I emerged victorious. He was mild when compared to Aurangzeb and sought to improve relations with the militant constituencies of the rapidly disintegrating kingdom. With time, he might have revived the imperial fortunes. Unfortunately, his death in 1712 plunged the empire once again into civil war.

Here too, an organisational parallel can be drawn. In family-run organisations occasionally a successor who is not aggressive enough is chosen because of the bloodline. This move then backfires. The opposite of this is when on occasion ultra-aggressive sales persons who exceed targets as individuals are promoted to managers to lead teams and they are unable to function effectively in this role since they are not able to come out of their aggressive, individual contributor mindset and work with the team and enable success in their team members.

During the time of the later Mughals, ambitious nobles became power brokers. Zulfiqar Khan, the Sayyid brothers and Nizam-ul-Mulkh were some such nobles who acquired dominant control over the affairs of the state. The last Mughal to exercise any real authority was Alamgir II. Alamgir's son Shah Alam II became

The Mughals After Aurangzeb

the first Mughal to live as a pensioner of the British. Shah Alam II's son Akbar II held the title of emperor but possessed neither money nor power.

Mughal kings after Aurangzeb relied on the nobles for not just the day-to-day affair of running the rule but extended their dependence on them even for strategic and military matters. The vastness of the kingdom would have required this delegation of authority. Delegating responsibility is an art, of being aware of 'what to delegate', 'whom to delegate' and 'how much to delegate'. Clearly, the later Mughals were inept at making these decisions. Relying solely on nobles was a major factor that led to the demise of the Mughal empire. The parallel can be drawn to weak corporate offices and powerful site offices that, if left unchecked, can destroy the organisation as it did the Mughal empire.

Yet another factor to consider was the financial position of the Mughals, which had become deplorable. The wars of succession, rebellions and the luxurious style of living depleted the once enormous treasury and led to financial bankruptcy. Thus, many factors and forces led to the fall of the Mughal empire. The final blow was dealt by a series of foreign invasions. Attacks by Nader Shah and Ahmad Shah Abdali almost destroyed Mughal military power. And finally, the emergence of the British challenged the last hope of revival. The role of a more agile and nimble competitor overthrowing an old, well established but moribund organisation is all too familiar!

For businesses, bouncing back after adversity is vital. Anger, disappointment, dejection, fear and there must have been other emotions that all the descendants of Aurangzeb might have experienced after each episode of adversity—be it internal conflicts for control or an overstretched empire with too many disgruntled subjects. But it did not translate into action.

Conclusion

It is not the purpose of this book to judge leaders. However, in the context of a continuing legacy, the Nizam and the descendants of Aurangzeb were unable to consolidate and build on what they inherited. In hindsight, we can always be very wise. That is the benefit of learning from history. No doubt, they may have many worthy contributions but from the perspective of building an organisation, we can learn from their errors.

In the case of the Nizam, putting his own interests ahead of those he ruled and taking a complex decision purely on the basis of emotions did not work. Being less emotional during such time separates good leaders from the mediocre ones. A good leader will always reflect on the decision, in a less emotional and professional manner, to judge whether the decision in correct or not. Being emotional while taking such decisions makes a leader ignore good ideas and settle for less.

Today, we are all in a hurry to run before we even walk. In this world, it becomes even more essential to learn from the descendants of Aurangzeb, and Aurangzeb himself, to pause, consolidate and then move on. Also, as we reach scale, we must learn to distribute work for long-term survival.

What other lessons can you learn?

Further Reading

M. Bhargava (ed.) *The Decline of the Mughal Empire* (Oxford University Press, 2014)

William Dalrymple, *The Last Mughal: The fall of a dynasty, Delhi, 1857*, (Bloomsbury, 2006)

Abraham Eraly, *Emperors of the Peacock Throne: The Saga of the Great Mughals* (Penguin, 2000)

Ramachandra Guha, *India after Gandhi: the History of the World's Largest Democracy* (Picador India, 2007)

K.N. Panikkar, *Towards Freedom: Documents on the Movement for Independence in India 1940: Part 2* (Oxford University Press, 2010)

N.S. Ramaswami, *Political History of Carnatic Under the Nawabs* (Abhinav, 1984)

Jadunath Sarkar, *A History of the Emperor Aurangzeb* (r.1658–1707 A.D.) Translated edn. Of Saqi Mustaid Khan's *Ma'asir-I Alamgiri* (Royal Society of Bengal, 1947)

Jadunath Sarkar, *The Fall of the Mughal Empire*, 4 vols. 2nd edition (South Asia Books, 1991–1992)

Mike Thomson, 'Hyderabad 1948: India's Hidden Massacre', BBC News, BBC, 24 September 2013, www.bbc.com/news/magazine-24159594.

John Zubrzycki, *The Last Nizam: an Indian Prince in the Australian Outback* (Pan Macmillan, 2007)

BROAD CONCLUSIONS

Having read these essays on different kinds of historical personalities, you will perhaps now agree that a couple of key themes surface:

- History is not about there being one 'right' way for things to happen. Humans are not always logical and are often a bundle of many contradictions. Due to this, 'right' or 'wrong' ways to do things don't always exist. Decisions and their outcomes are circumstantial. Carefully thought-out decisions may prove to be wrong in hindsight while random gambles may sometimes succeed. Still, there is much scope and material to take inspiration and learn from.
- Many historical sources are textual records written centuries ago. The writer does bring his or her own biases and views into the way they viewed and understood the events that transpired. Indeed, in every event, there is no one truth and while we may not agree or even approve of the other perspective, for those who hold contrary views, their opinion is valid and legitimate.
- If we keep aside the story of what happened and when, and instead look at why did people do or say what they did or said, history becomes relevant. This is so because our needs and fears and indeed human nature has not changed.

Broad Conclusions 149

The premise here is that human needs and fears (when needs are not met) are eternal and universal regardless of context. Money and technology only alter the way a need is met or a fear is created but they are never needs in themselves. There are also multiple needs and they may conflict with each other. Using this lens can make the history—of a region or a person—useful to understand and change behaviour to improve performance.

The focus of this book is to use history to alter one's own performance. I have therefore avoided any discussions on how to change the way the subject is taught or written.

Given that history proliferates around us, through observation and understanding, we can use it to help us perform better. This is a very economical and efficient way to use information we already have for a powerful goal we want to achieve.

For us to use history to alter our performance, it is essential to alter our view about history. Instead of worrying about dates and events, if we understand why people did what they did and how they did it and if it helped them achieve what they wanted in their life and after, then this new lens can give us insights we can use to improve our performance.

In this book, the story of each historical personality was narrated from the point of view of what they did, and the possible needs that may have motivated them to undertake those actions. It was then followed by a discussion (not an assessment) on whether their actions fulfilled those needs in their lifetime and after. To establish the eternal and universal nature of needs and the application of history, examples from modern-day business were also considered.

Each person can derive many lessons from the book to consider whether they need to start-stop-continue what they are doing to improve their performance. I have discussed a few, but if you have a friend who can also read the chapters, then a free-flowing discussion on the various themes identified can help you create a clear action plan of what you will say and do differently based on the lessons of leadership from the historical personalities discussed in the book.

A few suggested steps have been outlined in the next section to make that discussion more connected to your performance.

Sadhana: Using this book to examine beliefs and alter behaviour

Most management and self-help books are easy to read and agree with, but their ideas are difficult to put into practice. Perhaps the mistake is that we try to change in a day what we have been doing for a lifetime. Oftentimes we try to change behaviour by making to-do lists, practising 'positive thinking' or any of the latest management fads. These end up like new year resolutions, seldom lasting for more than a few weeks.

How then can we make sadhana or practice a more permanent, long-term feature that changes behaviour and helps us improve performance?

The key is in partnering with another person, a sakhi (friend/companion), who will offer non-judgemental but candid support and accompany you rather than lead or follow you in the journey.

Some rules that have been helpful to others who have been guided in this process:

1. Once you have picked a person, have a chat and agreement of how you are going to read the book, make notes and schedule future discussions.
2. Share some information with each other to build trust and help each other understand what biases may come as

Broad Conclusions

you read each chapter so that the other person watches out for them.

3. Discuss lessons from each chapter, look at how similar or different the needs and fears are, the connection to your performance context and what you can start, stop or continue. Take the help of the sakhi to avoid bias and make an action plan that can be measured and observed.
4. In subsequent meetings, discuss progress on your action plan, discuss reflective questions at the end of each chapter and how from that you can learn to examine your behaviour and beliefs.
5. Rather than looking at changing behaviour, if at first you just observe how many times the behaviour is occurring, you will automatically become more aware and self-correcting. That is the power of history! If we see it as relevant to our belief and behaviour, it will help us to change.
6. Make some notes about the experience. As you discuss the chapter and each question at the end of each chapter, connect both your responses to what you know of each other's life histories. Then contemplate on how you can use your own life history and that of your friend and the chapter to enhance your own performance.
7. Feel free to revisit chapters and discuss ways in which you can actively support each other as you look at behaviour change as well.

In this manner, you can use your history, your friend's history and Indian history to look deeply at your beliefs and alter your behaviour to improve your connection, contribution and legacy.

A WORD OF THANKS

This book would not have been possible without the inspiration I received from my teachers in school, college and university. They inspired in me a love for history and a curiosity to look at the same thing in different ways.

My colleagues in Infosys and McKinsey and other friends like T.T. Srinath, Kumaar Priyaranjan , N.V. Balachandar, Paul Abraham, Raghu Ananthanarayanan were all instrumental in helping me develop as a sensitive facilitator to understand history from a different perspective.

Jai Hiremath of Hikal, Vipul Tuli of Sembcorp and Vinod Dasari, then with Ashok Leyland, were leaders who were willing to trust me to implement the workshops based on history and leadership from which the insights for this book were born. If not for them, these would have just been ideas that lack proof!

Jay Ashar, Kaustubh Chakraborty, Nandan Kaushik, Sampath Kumar, Rajiv Lochan, Abarna Muthiah, Shruti Pillai and Bhargav Raghu were very helpful with reading and commenting on early drafts and helping me with references.

Karthik Venkatesh, my editor, and the team at Westland who have published this book also deserve my thanks.

My father S. Chakravarthy and my son, Raghavan are the pillars of support in my life. I owe them thanks in ways I cannot articulate in words!

With gratitude,
Pradeep Chakravarthy
pradeepchakravarthy75@gmail.com